Praise for *Joy...*

"This wonderful bo[...] [i]nformed by activist experience, emphasizes [...] [im]portance of the full range of political affects. Anger and rage rightly, inevitably drive militants, the authors argue, but we must also discover joy and friendship in struggle, which are our highest rewards. The book provides not only an antidote for anyone who has suffered the pitfalls of political activism but also a guide to a fulfilling militant life."

—Michael Hardt, co-author of *Assembly*

"The resurgence of the reactionary right has led many on the left to feel overwhelming despair. Resisting the rising tide of dread, this unique, genre-bending book offers a spirited defense of a militant politics of joy—an affirmative theory of openness and experimentation, curiosity and questioning. This is a thought-provoking, morale-boosting, hope-inspiring tonic offered at the moment we need it most."

—Astra Taylor, author of *The People's Platform*

"Combining humility, deep insight and open, liberatory theoretical foundations, *Joyful Militancy* importantly, and accessibly, asks hard questions and challenges the rigid culture within activism and social movements that need it. Instead with open hearts and minds the pages within offer thoughts for liberatory openings, not more answers, for all of us to explore within ourselves to radically engage in shifts from rigidity towards joy with sharp edges. This book kicks ass!"

—scott crow, author of *Black Flags and Windmills*

"Yes, yes, yes! This book is so timely! Absolutely what we need in these days of spreading gloom. A very well-argued case for joyful militancy, and against the dead hand of puritanical revolution. Read it, live it!"

—John Holloway, author of *Crack Capitalism*

"People who talk about revolution and class struggle without referring explicitly to everyday life, without understanding what is subversive about Joyful Militancy and what is positive in the affective refusal of Empire, such people have a corpse in their mouth. Nick Montgomery and carla bergman help us to remove that corpse so that we can sing new subversive songs, which is precisely what is needed more than ever."

—Stevphen Shukaitis, author of *The Composition of Movements to Come*

JOYFUL
MILITANCY

BUILDING RESISTANCE IN TOXIC TIMES

© 2017 Nick Montgomery and carla bergman
This edition © 2017 AK Press (Chico, Oakland, Edinburgh, Baltimore)

ISBN: 978-1-84935-288-8
E-ISBN: 978-1-84935-289-5
Library of Congress Control Number: 2017936236

AK Press   AK Press
370 Ryan Ave. #100   33 Tower St.
Chico, CA 95973   Edinburgh EH6 7BN
USA   Scotland
www.akpress.org   www.akuk.com
akpress@akpress.org   ak@akedin.demon.co.uk

Institute for Anarchist Studies
PO Box 90454
Portland, OR 97290
www.anarchiststudies.org

The above addresses would be delighted to provide you with the latest AK Press distribution catalog, which features books, pamphlets, zines, and stylish apparel published and/or distributed by AK Press. Alternatively, visit our websites for the complete catalog, latest news, and secure ordering.

Series design by Josh MacPhee / justseeds.org
Cover illustration and interior artwork by Pete Railand
Printed in the USA on acid-free, recycled paper

JOYFUL
MILITANCY

BUILDING RESISTANCE IN TOXIC TIMES

Nick Montgomery & carla bergman

Foreword by Hari Alluri

AK Press / Institute for Anarchist Studies | 2017

To everyone in cramped spaces and stifling atmospheres
letting in fresh air and finding wiggle room
embracing messiness and mistakes together
learning to move with fierce love and uncertainty
making us capable of something new

Anarchist Interventions:

An IAS/AK Press Book Series

Radical ideas can open up spaces for radical actions by illuminating hierarchical power relations and drawing out possibilities for liberatory social transformations. The Anarchist Intervention series—a collaborative project between the Institute for Anarchist Studies (IAS) and AK Press—strives to contribute to the development of relevant, vital anarchist theory and analysis by intervening in contemporary discussions. Works in this series will look at twenty-first-century social conditions—including social structures and oppression, their historical trajectories, and new forms of domination, to name a few—as well as reveal opportunities for different tomorrows premised on horizontal, egalitarian forms of self-organization.

Given that anarchism has become the dominant tendency within revolutionary milieus and movements today, it is crucial that anarchists explore current phenomena, strategies, and visions in a much more rigorous, serious manner. Each title in this series, then, will feature a present-day anarchist voice, with the aim, over time, of publishing a variety of perspectives. The series' multifaceted goals are to cultivate anarchist thought so as to better inform anarchist practice, encourage a culture of public intellectuals and constructive debate within anarchism, introduce new generations to anarchism, and offer insights into today's world and potentialities for a freer society.

Contents

Foreword by Hari Alluri

Willing to be Troubled: an essay with a love note to Gil Scott-Heron

We've all heard so many conflicting words
About life, whether wrong or right
How you gotta be workin' hard
And it ain't no easy job
To survive. Just keep it alive
                              —Gil Scott-Heron, "Willing"

Like the moment when I first heard Gil Scott-Heron, I knew upon first read that I would return to this book. The isolations of capitalism and the despairs of facing Empire's increasingly blatant yet always insidious machinations, oppressions, and attacks will drive me to seek the reminders that are here: of how to recognize my own moments of rigidity, and of how to recognize—beside, within, and far from me—moments of transformation. Though written by two white folks with deeply different experiences than Gil—folks who crucially implicate not just their privileges but also their behaviors—this book, like the song "Willing" quoted above, offers the echoes of sparks that pull me through lamentation toward reflection and action. Against the types of moments that, within movements, can lead to a "loss of collective power," both song and book offer me images of radical folks engaged in outright and everyday acts of resistance. They let me glance back, not nostalgically but gladly, at the faces of folks in my own communities actively supporting each other in radical friendships and lives whose resemblance to mainstream representations of happiness is only cursory: because there is a strength I see there that comes from— as carla bergman and Nick Montgomery identify it—the type of joy that looks and feels like growing more power- ful together.

This book troubles the second line of Gil Scott- Heron's "Willing," a song that, like much of his most powerful and resonant work, itself carries an air of trou- bling. *Joyful Militancy* called me back to this song and also through it because the project of this book is to move beyond "wrong or right" into a space of ethical question- ing that is always already conflicting yet, while shifting, can also be strong ground on which to build. As bergman and Montgomery identify in their introduction, "rigid radical- ism" stifles productive tension and risk-taking by tending "towards mistrust and fixed ways of relating that destroy the capacity to be responsive, creative, and experimental."

They continue astutely, refusing to fix "joyful militancy" as an ideal, thinking of it instead as "a fierce commitment to emergent forms of life in the cracks of Empire, and the values, responsibilities, and questions that sustain them." The structure and focus of the book are both attentive to moments of slippage and to regenerative practices. Because of this, I recall again listening to Gil Scott-Heron. I am thinking now of live versions of songs played with a full band that slip into and out of long and beautiful minutes of improvisation, especially versions of "The Bottle" in which Gil identifies the rhythm as Guan Guanco, "the rhythm of rebirth and regeneration" that survived the middle passage, a rhythm whose timing, like Gil's lyric tenacity from "The Revolution Will Not Be Televised" through "The Bottle" to "Willing" and beyond, can be troubling even as it cycles. One of the most powerful elements of *Joyful Militancy* is its commitment to remaining ever troubled: because no single program can give us the comfort of handing over to it the burdens of the work itself; because to remain troubled is to sustain a space of movement; because so many movements offer examples of a potential beauty that is itself improvised and cyclical.

This book is about connections, about echoes. It is built, as "Willing" is, on an acknowledgment of uninter-rupted survival and resistance. In choosing examples of movements and moments in which people offer everyday and organized versions of joyful militancy, bergman and Montgomery remind us that, despite all attempts to eradi-cate dissent, despite genocides and pogroms and police attacks and surveillance and micro-aggressions and the

myriad ways in which we hurt each other, we are uninter-
rupted. We are always already in conversation with movements and moments of the past that were themselves about
growing more powerful together, having each others' backs,
resisting corrosive practices while retrieving supportive
ones, choosing to work and grow in friendships less rusted
by the imperatives of capitalism and Empire: "There are—
and there always have been—many places and spaces where
alternatives are in full bloom."

Crucially, this book begins inside movement spaces,
spaces in which critiques of colonization, capitalism, and
Empire already exist: bergman and Montgomery are not
set out to convince a non-radicalized audience of the need
to resist. Rather, combining rigor with accessibility, they
affirm the lineages and contemporary currents of radical
thought and practice they draw from while acknowledging
the historical violence that made and make them necessary.
Echoing Rebecca Solnit, they state, "Everyday life under
Empire is already a certain kind of disaster." In a time when
"anarchist" is treated by too many as an empty epithet, in a
time when the most vulnerable communities are being targeted with cruelty, they openly state that "for joy to flourish, it needs sharp edges."

This book's opening urge is to respond to the affective
imperatives of what the authors term *rigid radicalism*:

> It is the pleasure of feeling more radical than oth-
> ers and the worry about not being radical enough;
> the sad comfort of sorting unfolding events into
> dead categories; the vigilant perception of errors

and complicities in oneself and others; the anxious posturing on social media and the highs of being liked and the lows of being ignored; the suspicion and resentment felt in the presence of something new; the way curiosity feels naïve and condescension feels right.

Affect is easily one of the more under-attended drivers of recent world events beyond and within movements, and it may also be among the most crucial spaces of intervention. The description above reminds me of despair, the despair I felt at times from Gil Scott-Heron that ached and aches me the most. At times, Gil seems to despair that his audience does not quite hear, does not quite grasp his message. It is precisely my own potential for this specific type of despair that I feel bergman and Montgomery help me combat, because it is a form of despair that is to the benefit of Empire. It is a despair that, in my experience, leads to isolation. When Gil passed on, friends, most of whom I had first met through different movements and organizations, reached out. I experienced a solidarity from them that was joyful in the sense of being co-realized, even as I was steeped in grief at the loss of an ancestor. As bergman and Montgomery note, "The self-enclosed individual is a fiction of Empire, just like the State. 'I' am already a crowd, enmeshed in others."

More widely, in conversation and collaboration with friends, with folks of divergent yet in-solidarity movements, they offer invocations instead of correctives. The authors accurately declare that ancient ways of growing more powerful together are always alive in the experiments of our activisms and our lives. bergman and Montgomery have at the same time a deep sense of how differences are necessary—of how specific oppressions we have faced position us to question, to offer that which other positions cannot—and of how our movements have built and can build from the small overlaps and resonances, not just because we all carry multiple identities but because certain common notions as well as differences we hold can bring us to have each others' backs.

bergman and Montgomery move by questions and attempts at response, noting how "common notions can only be held gently, as flexible, living ideas that are powerful in and through the relationships and processes they sustain." They converse with Black liberation, anti-violence, queer, youth, anarchist, and Indigenous resurgence movements. Theirs is something of a poetics: reminders and troublings of that which is always already present, whether in terms of the rigid radicalism that so often decays relationships within and between movements or in terms of identifying, supporting, and learning from moments and movements of empowered and empowering resistance. They offer a reading and imagining of empowerment that is Spinoza-inflected, anarchist-inflected, solidarity-inflected joy. Noting their own process, they acknowledge, "Neither of us could have written this book, or anything like it, alone. And the collaboration has made us each more capable, in different ways, together."

As I write this, my love—after a morning drawing fists on butcher paper to paste to placards—has gotten to her sister's to help their mom with caregiving for the babies. Her militancy, while divergent from the politics of some of her family, is steeped in an ethic of invitation and sharing that she learned from them, and right now our niece is coloring in a cutout of a brown fist almost as large as her. This is another version of the troubled and beautiful messiness that bergman and Montgomery remind me of in *Joyful Militancy*. I am thankful for it even as I sit with my grief at the present political moment and my urge to activate and be activated by those I love and those I've never met who, though far, are never quite distant.

Dear Gil,
Lolo, thank you for offering me moments of militant experimentation and troubled joy. For your work's anticipation of the growth of anti-apartheid solidarity with the people of South Africa. For when, decades later, many took to social media to reach out to you and, still willing in your final year of life, you heard their call and took up anti-apartheid solidarity with the people of Palestine. For so many moments that preceded them, moved between them, and followed them— moments of insight, moments of despair, moments of joy. At times, my most urgent desire is to feel untroubled. Thank you for divesting me from it over and over. Here, Gil, are some words that trouble me and offer me hope, some words that, like your words below, in shifting from individual to collective, in invoking the work and joy of generations, move me to tears: "For us at least, there is no cure, no gas mask, no unitary solution: there are only openings, searchings, and the collective discovery of new and old ways of moving that let in fresh air.

For the same reason that no one is immune, anyone can participate in its undoing."

Love,

Hari Alluri, on Kumeyaay land, January 20, 2017

"What my life really means is that the songs that I sing
Are just pieces of a dream that I've been building
And we can make a stand and hey, I'm reachin' out my hand
'Cause I know damn well we can if we are willing
But we gotta be ..."

("Willing," from the album *1980*)

Acknowledgments

We want to begin by thanking Richard Day for his ongoing guidance, friendship, and concrete support as our first editor, who waded through the manuscript (twice!) at its roughest and for working *with* us both with incredible openness, rigor, patience, care, and love throughout our entire process. And for his introduction to the very concept of joyful militancy—much gratitude for that because we wouldn't have written this book without him.

Thank you to Hari Alluri, poet, friend, militant about joy, joyfully militant kin! Deep gratitude for his careful and deeply generous edits to our book; his delight in the ideas, and his keen eye and brilliance all created the space for us both to take risks, to go toward our fear and speak more fiercely. We also want to celebrate his beautifully poignant foreword, thank you—words fail us on how to express our gratitude to him; we are honored and deeply indebted to him for all he has given to us and to this book.

Thank you to our editors at the Institute for Anarchist Studies (IAS) and Paul Messersmith-Glavin for supporting us through the first steps; thank you to Maia Ramnath for taking the final steps of shepherding the book into its final form with incredible generosity and incisiveness as our editor. Thanks to the 2013 IAS collective board for giving us the grant that got us going, and thanks to Cindy Milstein for encouraging us early on. Much gratitude to current IAS folks for continuing to support this project as it shifted and changed and emerged—special thanks to Kristian Williams, Chris Dixon, and Tamara Myers.

Thank you to Josh MacPhee, our generous and talented book designer who chose the perfect cover art. The cover illustration and art throughout the book is by the incredible Pete Railand: thanks to him for sharing his radical and relevant works with us. Thank you to AK Press, specifically Zach Blue and Charles Weigl, for helping us get here and turning our book into a thing made of paper!

Thanks to our incredibly generous interviewees, whose ideas shaped and morphed our book immeasurably. Immense gratitude goes out to Silvia Federici, adrienne maree brown, Marina Sitrin, Gustavo Esteva, Kelsey Cham C., Zainab Amadahy, Leanne Betasamosake Simpson, Melanie Matining, Sebastian Touza, Walidah Imarisha, Mik Turje, Margaret Killjoy, Tasnim Nathoo, Glen Coulthard, and Richard Day.

And many thanks to all the folks who had informal conversations with us about our book, in particular thank you to Kim Smith, Rebecca Solnit, Klee Benally, and Astra Taylor.

Thank you to Dana Putnam for generously offering up her home for a writing retreat.

Thank you to the Zapatistas for changing the narrative

and busting the hegemonic hold on our Western imaginations of what new worlds could look like. Thanks to Gustavo Esteva for making connections long ago and shining a bright light on the road as we try to write about similar ideas.

bell hooks, for busting it all up and offering love. Ivan Illich for providing language to write about concepts one mostly feels. Baruch Spinoza, for asking what a body can do. Gilles Deleuze for offering new ways to believe in the world. Marina Sitrin, horizontal trailblazer and speaker of love and generous spirit, thank you! Audre Lorde for foregrounding the subversive power of desire and feeling. John Holloway for helping us to imagine the possibility of an active, radical (sometimes raging) hope. And thanks to Sebastian Touza for engaging with us about common notions in his work and offering us incredible feedback.

Thanks to everyone building worlds, making and defending kin, supporting flourishing, walking with questions, staying with the trouble.

Nick's acknowledgments:

Collaborating on this book has been a transformative experience and also a difficult one. Writing is hard for me unless I am doing little else, so writing a whole book meant withdrawing from a lot of the conversations, activities, and currents that have inspired this work. It has meant becoming disconnected, at least partially, from a lot of the things that challenge, fuel, and undo me in enabling ways. It sometimes felt weird to write about the importance of friendship, trust, and collective transformation as I became more isolated from many of the relationships that have taught me about all this.

For that reason, among many others, I want to express deep gratitude to my friends, housemates, my partner, my family, and everyone close to me who has continued to reach out. Words inevitably fail here, and I hope I can show you some of the gratitude I feel.

Thanks to Kim Smith for all the ways you've supported me and taught me about thinking, vulnerability, trust, ambivalence, care, and challenge, and for your inspiring and infectious capacity to hold complexity and find potential in hopelessness and tangled attachments. Thanks for renewing my interest in Spinoza and Deleuze several years ago (and teaching me so much about them), for helping me be curious, for endless stimulating conversations, and for reading early drafts and offering incisive comments and encouragement. Citations and acknowledgments can't really do justice to the ways you've shaped the ways I think and move, or to the ways this book has been shaped by our encounters.

Thanks to Seb Bonet and Jennine Downie for your incredible patience and support, for extending yourselves and/or shaking me in so many ways, and for inviting me into your lives and role-modeling intentionality and generosity, among many other things. Thanks, Sacha and Stella, for teaching me how to play again and for your fierce resistance to being treated like children. Thanks to other hyenas, past and present: Colton, Sharmarke, Jac, Fletch,

Mary, Mark, and Jesse for engaging in weird and wonderful experiments of collective living. Thanks to Isaac Rosenberg and Meg Neufeld for your encouragement and friendship, for reading early drafts, and for being present with me. Thanks to Richard Day and Joan Donaghey for your intellectual and material generosity, for being solid and messy at the same time, and for letting me hit my own head against many beams. Thanks to Bob Lovelace for offering teachings with relentless patience, humility, and care for people and place. Thanks to my MA supervisors Warren Magnusson and Rob Walker for teaching me, in different ways, to think patiently, impatiently, and deeply. Thank you, Ana Maria Peredo, for supporting me and others, and for creating convivial spaces within an academy that can be so isolating.

Thanks to friends, mentors, and collaborators, political and intellectual and intimate, for engaging in so many great experiments: JJ, Matt L, Danielle, trish, Dani, Gillian, Wulfgang, Kelsey, Daley, Bradley, Julie Anne, Joshua, Mik, Greg, Jennie, Captain, Jet, Carol, Eric, Noah, Jenny, Katie, and so many other influences and supports and inspirations, too numerous to name. Thanks to all the incredible collaborators and mentors in the Anti-Violence Project, OUST, the UVic Men's Circle, Camas, the People's Apothecary, Dinner for Troubled Times, Food Not Lawns, GRAFT, the Social Spaces Summit, the Purple Thistle Institute, and other quieter experiments.

Thanks, Jeanette Sheehy, for exploring so much of this with me early on, for grappling with patriarchy and sad militancy before we had words for them, for centering friendship, and for continuing to inspire me with your

weirdness and spikiness. Thanks for having the courage to
sever ties when they no longer served us and remake them
when they did.

Thanks to my sister Jesse for her consistent love, kindness, and incredible humour. Thanks to my parents, Rick
Montgomery and Susan Baker, for decades of uncondition-
al love and support, even when my choices and commitments seemed baffling. Thanks for your willingness to let
me explore and make my own mistakes, and for all the ways
you've helped me thrive through struggle and grappling
with thriving.

carla, thank you for role-modeling joy and conviviality and helping me orient to it, and for gently helping me
unlearn the ways that sadness and rigidity suffused so much
of the ways I went about organizing, relationships, and
theory. Thanks for your fierce kindness, spikey commitments, awe-inspiring intuition, and the incredible ways you
nurture and tend relationships (including ours!). Thanks to
Chris, Zach, and Lilah for hosting me countless times, sharing space with me, and being open and welcoming in ways
that made me feel like I somehow always already belonged
among you (thanks also to the red couch in the bunker!)

carla has a few folks to give her deep gratitude to:

I have to begin by thanking my philosophy prof from
back in the day because he loved Spinoza and introduced
me to his work. There are so many people, like my college
prof, who are of all ages, who have inspired and supported

this work—many of whom stretch back my entire life (50 years!). So generally I want to express my deepest gratitude to all the encounters that brought joy and learning into my life – especially on the front lines of struggle. You're all in my heart. Thank you!

Thank you to the Purple Thistle Community—especially all the youth, Matt Hern, and Am Johal—I am forever grateful for all I experienced, the trouble we caused, and all the unlearning we did together. Thank you to the Common Notions Documentary crew, especially Corin Browne and John Collins. Making the film with you two at the same as writing this book was a gift!

I also want to share my deepest gratitude with: Gustavo Esteva for expanding my understanding of friendship and hospitality. Madhu Suri Prakash, for sharing your wisdom with me. Mike Davis, for inspiring me to write and your boundless kindness. Rebecca Solnit, for responding with an incredible amount of delight and encouragement. scott crow, for having an emergency and generous heart at a distance.

My east-van kin and friends, thank you, Anita, Emily, Kelley, Dana, Hiromi, Gin, Laura, Savanna, Meghan, Iris, Corin, Nicola, mia, LeyAnn, Vivienne, Carmen, Khelsilem, Selena, and Helen! I especially want to say thank you for supporting me (and my family) while I became less and less available for visits while I worked on this book. Thank you you all, sincerely, for sending along encouragement when I needed it most.

My Friends-Kin far away from here, thank you, Lily (and family), Maya, Tamara, Astra, Kelsey C, Dani,

Jeanette, Piers, Hari, Mike Jo, Richard, Melissa, Kim and Son, your generous encouragement and inspiration from a distance were and are a constant support.

Thank you to my sister, Candice Wright, for singing "Joy Will Find a Way" most of my life (and in extension a shout out to Bruce Cockburn for writing it).

For the concrete support during the book writing, my deepest of gratitude to: Julie Flett, for years of careful, gentle friendship (the shared love for our boys!) and modeling what it can look like to do meaningful creative works. Lisa Prentice, for our collaborative *healing journey* that worked with my body to be stronger. Tasnim Nathoo, for your grounded thoughts, your early readings of the book, and incredible advice. Sylvia McFadden, for deeply *feeling* what we mean when we say *Joy*—thank you for the ability to hold onto conflicting feelings and for making kin with us. My daughter and most favorite person in the world, Lilah Joy Bergman, for teaching me how to be in the moment and trust emerging powers, how to be kind and fierce, while setting solid boundaries, and how to love my friends with my whole heart—I am still learning. My son, my muse, and bestest friend of all time, Zach Francis, for teaching me how to trust, how to support autonomy and self-determination while also being solid and caring. Thank you for walking with me and teaching me about pace and keeping me (somewhat) cool by teaching me about rad aesthetics and sound-art. Chris Bergman, my partner, a wizard, a patriarchy buster, and my other best friend for the past 25 years, thank you for loving me unconditionally all these years, for undoing with me all along the way, and in the best way possible. Eternal gratitude for bringing laughter and play front and center into our life and helping me see and feel the wonderment in the everyday!

Nick, thank you for saying YES! when I suggested that we write something about Joyful Militancy back in 2013; I could have *never* written this book without you, but you know that. Thank you for almost always traveling to me and making collaboration accessible in doing so. But mostly thank you for trusting me, making kin with us at the bunker, and holding and supporting me through a big barrier of mine. Your kindness and openness, your desire to work through the hard parts and celebrate the small joys are all inspiring, contagious, and deeply appreciated.

And finally, from us both, much gratitude to Chris Bergman for feeding us good food and taking care of us in many other concrete and subtle ways while we wrote this book. You are an embodiment of much of what we write and affirm in this book, and we love you.

Introduction

There are no new ideas. There are only new ways of making them felt.

—Audre Lorde[1]

People who talk about revolution and class struggle without referring explicitly to everyday life, without understanding what is subversive about love and what is positive in the refusal of constraints—such people have a corpse in their mouth.

—Raoul Vaneigem[2]

Do not think that one has to be sad in order to be a militant, even though the thing one is fighting is abominable.

—Michel Foucault[3]

This book is an attempt to amplify some quiet conversations that have been happening for a long time, about the connections between resisting and thriving, about how we relate to each other in radical movements today, and about some of the barriers to collective transformation.

There is something that circulates in many radical movements and spaces, draining away their transformative potential. Anyone who has frequented these spaces has felt it. Many (including us) have actively participated in it, spread it, and been hurt by it. It nurtures rigidity, mistrust, and anxiety precisely where we are supposed to feel most alive. It compels us to search ourselves and others ruthlessly for flaws and inconsistencies. It crushes experimentation and curiosity. It is hostile to difference, complexity, and nuance. Or it is the *most* complex, the most nuanced, and everyone else is simplistic and stupid. Radicalism becomes an *ideal*, and everyone becomes deficient in comparison.

The anxious posturing, the vigilant search for mistakes and limitations, the hostility that crushes a hesitant new idea, the way that critique becomes a reflex, the sense that things are urgent yet pointless, the circulation of the latest article tearing apart bad habits and behaviors, the way shaming others becomes comfortable, the ceaseless generation of necessities and duties, the sense of feeling guilty about one's own fear and loneliness, the clash of political views that requires a winner and a loser, the performance of anti-oppressive language, the way that some stare at the floor or look at the door. We know these tendencies, intimately. We have seen them circulating and felt them pass through us.

When we began talking with friends about this, there were immediate head nods and sometimes excited eruptions—"Yes! *Finally* someone is going to talk about this publicly!" No one knew exactly what it was or where it came from, but many knew exactly what we were talking about. Like us, they had felt it and participated in it. They had discussed it quietly and carefully with people they trusted. But it was hard to unpack, for a whole bunch of reasons. To complain or criticize it came with the risk of being attacked, shamed, or cast out. This phenomenon is difficult to talk about because it presents itself as the *most* radical, the *most* anti-oppressive, the *most* militant. It shape-shifts and multiplies itself: sometimes it appears as one rigid line, at other times as a proliferation of positions arrayed against each other. How is it that explicitly radical, anti-oppressive, or anti-authoritarian spaces—the places where people should feel most alive and powerful—can sometimes feel cold, stifling, and rigid? What contributes to a climate in which one is never radical enough, where we have to continually prove our radicalness to others? What makes insecurity, distrust, anxiety, guilt, and shame so pervasive? Where does all this come from? What is this thing? Is it one thing or many? What activates it, stokes it, and how can it be warded off?

We are not the first to try to get ahold of this phenomenon. It has gone by many names—*sad militancy*, *grumpy-warriorcool*, *manarchism*, *puritanism*—each of which emphasizes different elements and sources. In this book, we call it *rigid radicalism.* Our research and experience lead us to think that its origins are as diverse as the phenomenon itself. Some say rigid radicalism comes from the way heteropatriarchy poisons intimacy with trauma and violence, while separating politics from everyday life. Others point to origins in the narcissistic and guilt-ridden individualism nurtured by whiteness. Or it is the way schooling replaces creativity and curiosity with conformity and evaluation. Or the humiliation of a life organized by capitalism, in which we are all pitted in petty competitions with each other. Or the way cynicism evolves from attempts to avoid pain and failure. Or it is identity politics fused with neoliberalism. And the terror and anxiety of a world in crisis. And the weakening of movements and a decline in militancy. Or it is the existence of radical milieus as such. And the deep insecurity nurtured by social media and its injunction to public performance. Or it is morality or ideology or the Left or the Maoists or the nihilists or the moralists or the ghost of Lenin. Probably there is some truth to all of these: it is definitely a tangled web.

It is important to say, from the outset, that we do *not* think the problem is simply anger, conflict, or difference. Whenever people name and challenge oppression and violence, there are almost always reactionaries telling them they are doing it wrong, that they need to be polite, nice, reasonable, peaceful, or patient. We want nothing to do with attempts to regulate resistance.

For this reason, we do not believe rigid radicalism can be countered by inventing a new set of norms for how to behave or setting out a new ideal of what radicalism should be. There can be no instructions. This would just create a new ideal to measure ourselves against. It would just add to a long list of shoulds, dos, and don'ts that reactivates the problem. We hope to help undo tendencies towards regulation and policing, rather than play into them.

Maybe we are stoking rigid radicalism right now, in writing about it. Searching out its roots and inner workings can re-create a stifling atmosphere in which we feel like we are stuck, always lacking, always messing up, with no escape. Pointing to shame, rigidity, guilt, competition, or anxiety does not make them go away, and it might make things worse. It is not a question of revealing the fact that we don't treat each other well sometimes or that movements can turn in on themselves; we know this already. These tendencies are a public secret: widely known but difficult to talk about.[4] Tracing origins might not tell us much about what to do here and now. It is not about a few bad apples or a few bad behaviors. For us, at least, it cannot be reduced to *those people over there,* because we feel it arise in ourselves as well. There is no way to purify our movements of these tendencies because the desire for purity is part of the problem.

So our project is not about being *against* rigid radicalism. We have become convinced that rigid radicalism cannot be countered by critique alone. Our critique and interrogation are a way of asking: how can we be otherwise? What makes it possible to activate something different? How to protect the something different once it gains traction? How to share experiences of places and spaces where something different is already taking place—where people feel more alive and capable?

The first step, for us, has been to affirm that we are *already otherwise*: we all have parts of ourselves that are drawn towards other ways of being. Everyone has glimmers, at least, of the ways that fierceness can be intertwined with kindness, and curiosity with transformation. Every space is a complex ecology of different tendencies. Rigid radicalism is always only one tendency among others. There are—and always have been—many places and spaces where alternatives are in full bloom. Beyond merely diagnosing or combating rigid radicalism, we seek to affirm the multiplicity of ways that spaces can be otherwise.

QUESTIONS

This is part of what we have been talking about with people: What makes radical spaces and movements feel transformative and creative, rather than dogmatic, rule-bound, or stifling? What sustains struggles, spaces, and forms of life where we become capable of living and fighting in new ways? What supports people's capacities to challenge each other and undo deeply ingrained habits, rather than just saying the "right" thing or avoiding the "wrong" thing? How are people carving out relationships based in trust, love, and responsibility amid the violence that permeates daily life? What sustains these worlds—what makes them thrive?

With so much destruction in motion, this might all sound naïve to some readers: why speak of thriving and love when there are so many massive, urgent problems that need to be confronted? To write about the potential of trust and care, at this time in history, could seem like grasping optimistically at straws as the world burns. But durable bonds and new complicities are not a reprieve or an escape; they are the very means of undoing Empire.

We use "Empire" to name the organized destruction under which we live. Through its attempt to render everything profitable and controllable, Empire administers a war with other forms of life. The rhythms it imposes are at once absorptive and isolating. Even when this war takes the apparently subtle forms of assimilation and control, it is backed by brutal violence. Prisons and cops lurk alongside discourses of inclusion and tolerance. Empire works to monopolize the whole field of life, crushing autonomy and inducing dependence.

At the same time, there are cracks everywhere. A basic premise of this book is that resistance and transformation are always in the making at the margins, while Empire is always adapting and reacting. All of its mechanisms of control have been invented as responses to the constant upwelling of resistance, autonomy, and insurrection. This upwelling is a struggle not only against external domination, but also against Empire's control over identities, desires, and relationships. Undoing Empire also means undoing oneself. This is never a purely negative undoing, because it also means becoming capable of something new.

We are convinced that what is needed is an *activation* and *affirmation* of other ways of being. Not a new norm but the exploration of new (and old) capacities. This book explores some of these capacities alongside the ways that people are transforming their own situations without governments or hierarchical institutions. The capacity to treat each other well is connected, we think, to movements that nurture autonomy, trust, responsibility, and the collective power that is palpable when people are able to participate more fully in life. Amid and beyond barricades and Molotovs there are new forms of care and belonging, quiet and humble forms of support. There are emergent sensibilities based in listening, curiosity, and experimentation. There are reconnections with subjugated traditions and practices. There is hatred of the forces that threaten all this, and a willingness to fight. Some have been nurturing these capacities for a long time; others are just beginning to explore them. For this reason, rather than just dwelling in the pervasiveness of rigid radicalism or Empire, here we are exploring, celebrating, and connecting with other ways of being—other thriving forms of resistance and struggle.

AFFIRMATIVE THEORY

In many currents of radicalism—especially certain strains of Marxism—radical theory tasks itself with directing the course of struggle, pointing the way forward, or handing down instructions and fixed ways of being. This kind of theory generates necessities or suggestions to be implemented. Theory directs practice. Either this, or theory is tasked with critique of the world, of practice, and of other theories: it is supposed to reveal the limits of current struggles, discover the mistakes and flawed ways of doing or thinking, or reveal the root of oppression. Often both these modes of theory generate positions defined in opposition to others. They give us things to be *for* or *against*.

But there are other modes of theory. Theory can also explore connections and ask open-ended questions. It can affirm and elaborate on something people already intuit or sense. It can celebrate and inspire; it can move. We want a kind of theory that *participates* in struggle and the growth of shared power rather than directing it or evaluating it from outside. We are after a kind of theory that is critical but also affirmative. Rather than pointing to the limits or shortcomings of movements and declaring what they should do, affirmative theory homes in on the most transformative edges and margins.

In writing this book, we've been influenced by many divergent voices and movements, and we want to value them all. We combine weighty philosophical concepts with conversations and draw on zines, academic articles and books, speeches, and interviews. Furthermore, we think there's a lot to be said for bringing things together in unforeseen ways that might intensify their aliveness and dynamism. This entails asking and provoking questions, many of which we leave open and unresolved throughout the book. For us, the most compelling questions are those that can be answered in a multiplicity of ways, in different situations.

One of our basic premises is that transformative potentials are always already present and emergent. Not only *can* things be otherwise; they already *are,* and it is a matter of tuning, tending, activating, connecting, and defending these processes of change that are already in the making. People are always enacting alternatives to the dominant order of things, however small, and there are always new connections and potentials to explore. We see this kind of sensibility happening in currents of feminism, queer theory, Black liberation, Indigenous resurgence, youth liberation, anarchism, autonomism, and radical ecology, among others, and we seek to affirm these movements and practices throughout the book.

But this is tricky: how are we to affirm and explore spaces where something transformative is taking place without holding them up as ideals to imitate or telling others to be a certain way? What we are after is not a new critique or new position but a *process*. Not a new direction for movements but the process of movement itself and the growth of creativity, struggle, experimentation, and collective power.

JOY AND THE SPINOZAN CURRENT

> To reduce these problems to a complete and final analysis would be to miss the point. The best thing would be an informal discussion capable of bringing about the subtle magic of wordplay.
> It is a real contradiction to talk of joy seriously.
> —Alfredo Bonanno[5]

Pursuing these questions took us on a long detour through a minor current of Western philosophy associated with Baruch Spinoza. Against the grain of European thought that sought to subdue life through rigid dualisms and classifications, Spinoza conceptualized a world in which everything is interconnected and in process.

This worldview meant that Spinoza was despised by most of his contemporaries, but his ideas have influenced numerous currents of radical theory and practice, including anarchism, autonomous Marxism, affect theory, deep ecology, psychoanalysis, post-structuralism, queer theory, and even neuroscience. We are drawing on a current that runs from Spinoza through Friedrich Nietzsche, Gustav Landauer, Michel Foucault, and Gilles Deleuze to contemporary radicals like the Invisible Committee, Colectivo Situaciones, Lauren Berlant, Michael Hardt, and Antonio Negri. What we have found exciting about this current is the focus on processes through which people become more alive, more capable, and more powerful together. For Spinoza, the whole point of life is to become capable of new things, with others. His name for this process is joy.

Joy? What? Doesn't joy just mean happiness, with some vaguely Christian undertones? Later we'll be more precise about joy, but for now we want to be clear that it is not the same thing as happiness. A joyful process of transformation might *involve* happiness, but it tends to entail a whole range of feelings at once: it might feel overwhelming, painful, dramatic, and world-shaking, or subtle and uncanny. Joy rarely feels comfortable or easy, because it transforms and reorients people and relationships. Rather than the desire to exploit, control, and direct others, it is resonant with emergent and collective capacities to do things, make things, undo painful habits, and nurture enabling ways of being together.[6]

Moreover, Spinoza's concept of joy is not an emotion at all but an increase in one's power to affect and be affected. It is the capacity to do and feel more. As such, it is connected to creativity and the embrace of uncertainty. Within the Spinozan current, there is no way to determine what is right and good for everyone. It is not a moral philosophy, with a fixed idea of good and evil. There is no recipe for life or struggle. There is no framework that works in all places, at all times. What is transformative in one context might be useless or stifling in another. What worked once might become stale, or, on the other hand, the recovery of old memories and traditions might be enlivening. So does this mean anything goes? People just do what they want? Rejecting universal arbiters like morality and the state doesn't mean falling into "chaos" or "total relativity." The space beyond fixed and established orders, structures, and morals is not one of disorder: it is the space of *emergent* orders, values, and forms of life.

JOYFUL MILITANCY AND EMERGENT POWERS

When people come into contact with their own power— with their capacity to participate in something life-giving— they often become more militant. "Militancy" is a loaded word for some, evoking images of machismo and militarism. For us, militancy means combativeness and a willingness to fight, but fighting might look like a lot of different things. It might mean the struggle against internalized shame and oppression; fierce support for a friend or loved one; the courage to sit with trauma; a quiet act of sabotage; the persistence to recover subjugated traditions; drawing lines in the sand; or simply the willingness to risk. We are intentionally bringing joy and militancy together, with the aim of thinking through the connections between fierceness and love, resistance and care, combativeness and nurturance.

When people find themselves genuinely supported and cared for, they are able to extend this to others in ways that seemed impossible or terrifying before. When people find their bellies filled and their minds sharpened among communal kitchens and libraries, hatred for capitalist ways of life grows amid belonging and connection. When someone receives comfort and support from friends, they find themselves willing to confront the abuse they have been facing. When people develop or recover a connection to the places where they live, they may find themselves standing in front of bulldozers to protect that place. When people begin to meet their everyday needs through neighborhood assemblies and mutual aid, all of a sudden they are willing to fight the police, and the fight deepens bonds of trust and solidarity. Joy can be contagious and dangerous.

All over the world, there are stories of people who find themselves transformed through the creation of other forms of life: more capable, more alive, and more connected to each other, and willing to defend what they are building. In our conversations with others from a variety of currents and locations, we have become increasingly convinced that the most widespread, long-lasting, and fierce struggles are animated by strong relationships of love, care, and trust. These values are not fixed duties that can be imitated, nor do they come out of thin air. They arise from struggles through which people become powerful together. As people force Empire out of their lives, there is more space for kindness and solidarity. As people reduce their dependence on Empire's stifling institutions, collective responsibility and autonomy can grow. As people come to trust their capacity to figure things out together rather than relying on the state and capitalism, they are less willing to submit to the fears and divisions that Empire fosters.

These emergent powers are at the core of the Spinozan lineage, of this book, and (we think) of many vibrant movements today. Drawing on Spinoza, we call them *common notions*. To have a common notion is to be able to participate more fully in the web of relations and affections in which we are enmeshed. They are not about controlling things but about *response-ability*, capacities to remain responsive to changing situations. This is why they are a bit paradoxical: they are *material* ideas, accessed by tuning into the forces that compose us, inseparable from the feelings and practices that animate them. Abstract morality and ideology are barriers to this tuning-in, offering up rule-bound frameworks that close us off from the capacity to modulate the forces of the present moment.

Similarly, we have come to think that while trust is fundamental in transformative struggle, it cannot be an obligation; trust is always a gift and a risk. Common notions are inherently experimental and collective. They subsist by hanging onto uncertainty, similar to the Zapatistas' notion *preguntando caminamos*: "asking, we walk." For the same reason, common notions are always in danger of being stifled by rigid radicalism, which tends towards mistrust and fixed ways of relating that destroy the capacity to be responsive and inventive. Joyful militancy, then, is a fierce commitment to emergent forms of life in the cracks of Empire, and the values, responsibilities, and questions that sustain them.

||

BEYOND OPTIMISM AND PESSIMISM

While we want to insist that there are potentials bubbling up everywhere, it doesn't always feel that way. This is not an optimistic book. We are not interested in sacrificing the present for a revolution in the distance, nor are we confident that things will get better. They may get worse, for many of us, in many ways. However, we are equally wary of pessimism and cynicism. Among others, feminist essayist Rebecca Solnit has taught us to see optimism and pessimism as two sides of the same coin: both try to remove uncertainty from the world. Both foster certitude about how things will turn out, whether good or bad. Optimism and pessimism can provide a sense of comfort at the expense of openness and the capacity to hang onto complexity. They can drain away our capacity to care, to try, and to fight for things to be otherwise without knowing how it will turn out. A fundamental premise of this book is that no matter what, things *can* be otherwise—there is always wiggle room, Empire is already full of cracks, and the future is always uncertain. Uncertainty is where we need to begin, because experimentation and curiosity is part of what has been stolen from us. Empire works in part by making us feel impotent, corroding our abilities to shape worlds together.

In this book we hope to affirm a diverse array of struggles and alternatives in the making, including prison abolition and transformative justice, feminism and anti-violence, youth liberation, and Indigenous resurgence and land defense, among others. This kind of connection is less about adding up movements as if they could be unified, and more about illustrating the productiveness of their difference; like combining different tones and rhythms to see how they resonate.

To think and feel through this process, rather than creating new norms or positions, may be frustrating for some readers. It might sound a bit fluffy to insist that experimentation and struggle go hand in hand, or that celebration and love are linked to militant resistance. They aren't always connected. Yet creativity and experimentation are vital in the face of forces that not only crush disobedience but also steer desires. We want to affirm the ways that creative destruction and combative resistance can be linked to walking with questions, and all of this can make us more alive and capable together. Joyful militancy is a dangerous, transformative, and experimental process, generated collectively and held gently.

ON ANARCHISM

"Q: if an anarcho-syndicalist, an insurrectionary anarchist, and an anarcho-primitivist are sitting together in the back of a car, who's driving?

A: A cop!"

This book is also an intervention into anti-authoritarian movements, especially anarchism. Many threads of anarchism infuse our lives and the lives of those we care about, and we have been inspired and influenced by a range of different anti-authoritarian currents. At its most vibrant, anarchism is not an ideology but a creative rejection of the ideologies of the state, capitalism, and the Left. Crucial to anarchism is the attempt to escape the certainties of Empire *and* the certainties that can arise in struggle. Anarchism can support a trust in people's capacities to figure out for themselves how to live and fight together rather than constructing a model or blueprint for resistance. Whereas dominant currents of Marxism and liberalism assume the necessity of the state and activate desires for unity and sameness, anarchism often nurtures autonomy, decentralization, and difference.

The anarchism we are interested in does not tell us what we should do. For us this is crucial. Anarchism can help us inhabit spaces by trusting our own capacities and relating in ways that are emergent and responsive to change. But as with any other tradition, anarchism can also crystallize into a fixed ideology. It can produce closed and stifling milieus. It can lead to duty-bound collectivism or simplistic individualism. It can feel like a club whose boundaries are policed or a badge to display one's radical cred. Anarchist spaces can feel cold, unwelcoming, and scary. Anyone familiar with anarchist milieus knows that there can be vicious sectarian conflicts, which often entrench rigid loyalties and positions.

We do not focus much on these debates here, nor do we situate ourselves as particular types of anarchists. This is partly because we have learned from many different currents, and it seems counterproductive to elevate one above the others. We also want to avoid some of the debates that, to us, have become sedimented and stale. At its best, we think, anarchism nurtures trust in people's capacity to figure things out, while also supporting autonomy and leaving room for conflict. We are inspired by all the ways that anarchists are able to inhabit situations with strong values and fierce care, while also respecting and even welcoming difference.

We are particularly interested in currents of anarchism and anti-authoritarianism that have emphasized the importance of affinities over ideologies. Affinity is a helpful concept for us because it speaks to emergent relationships and forms of organizing that are decentralized and flexible but not flimsy. Organizing by affinity basically means seeking out and nurturing relationships based in shared values, commitments, and passions, without trying to impose those on everyone else. Affinity is also important because many of the currents that inspire us either reject anarchism—along with all other "isms"—or just don't have much interest in it. Some of the people we interviewed are self-proclaimed anarchists who are known in anarchist milieus. Others have been deeply influenced by anarchism, and it inflects their projects and their lives, but they don't identify much with the political label. Others have traditions of autonomy and resistance that come from other sources, including Indigeneity and other non-Western traditions. For many, resistance to hierarchy, violence, and exploitation has been something intuitive or a question of

survival. They are forcing Empire out of their lives and linking up with others doing the same.

There is a conversation going on, within and beyond
anarchism, about the potential of strong relationships that
are rooted in trust, love, care, and the capacity to support
and defend each other. The most exciting currents of anarchism, for us, are those that encourage and enable people
to live differently here and now, and to break down divides
between organizing and everyday life.

THE BEGINNING OF A CONVERSATION

How can these processes of transformation be nurtured
and defended, not just in their most dramatic and exceptional moments, but all the time? Are there common values
or sensibilities that nurture transformative relationships,
alive and responsive to changing situations, while warding
off both Empire and rigid radicalism? What if joy (as the
process of becoming more capable) was seen as fundamental to undoing Empire? What would it mean to be *militant*
about joy? What is militancy when it is infused with creativity and love?

It was with these questions—much vaguer and more
muddled at the time—that the two of us began having intentional conversations with several others. And
who are we, the two of us? Both of us live in so-called
British Columbia, Canada—Nick in Victoria and carla
in Vancouver. We come from different generations, and
we have pretty different life experiences across gender,
class, ability, and education. carla has been involved in

deschooling, youth liberation organizing, and other radical currents for a couple of decades now, and she became a mentor to Nick several years ago as Nick was realizing that he was a radical in his mid-twenties without many mentors from older generations (a common phenomenon in anarchist and other radical worlds). What began as a relationship of mentorship and political collaboration evolved into a deep friendship. In terms of our organizing, we are both oriented towards prefigurative experiments: trying to contribute to projects and forms of life where we are able to live and relate differently with others here and now, and supporting others doing the same. Both of us are white cisgendered settlers, and for us this has meant trying to write in conversation with people with very different life experiences and insights, including Indigenous people, kids and youth, Black people and other folks of color, and genderqueer and trans folks, all of whom struggle against forms of violence and oppression that we can never know. We have also sought to talk with people from a wide variety of movements in many different places throughout Turtle Island (North America) and Latin America.

Over the course of a year and a half we spoke with friends and friends of friends. This was a unique research process, in part because we were inviting people into an ongoing conversation, asking them to reflect on and respond to our continually evolving ideas about joyful militancy and rigid radicalism. We formally interviewed fifteen people in all: Silvia Federici, adrienne maree brown, Marina Sitrin, Gustavo Esteva, Kelsey Cham Corbett, Zainab Amadahy, Leanne Betasamosake Simpson, Melanie Matining, Tasnim

Nathoo, Sebastian Touza, Walidah Imarisha, Mik Turje, Margaret Killjoy, Glen Coulthard, and Richard Day. We also had many more informal conversations with folks from a lot of different backgrounds, of all ages, who impacted our thinking immensely.

These people are not representatives of any particular group or movement. Nor are we holding them up as the ultimate embodiment of joy, militancy, or radicalism. They are people with whom we share values and who inspire and challenge us. All of them are committed, in various ways, to forcing Empire out of their lives and reviving and nurturing other worlds. They are involved in a diversity of movements, struggles, and forms of life: the uprisings in Oaxaca and Argentina; small-scale farming and urban food justice; Black liberation and prison abolition; Indigenous resurgence and land defense; transformative and healing justice movements; radical ecology and permaculture; scavenging and squatting; youth liberation and deschooling; feminist and anti-violence work; the creation of autonomous, queer, BIPOC spaces;[7] direct action and anticapitalist organizing, and much more, including the beautiful and fierce ways of being that are difficult to capture in words. Experiences among the people we interviewed ranged widely, from long-term commitments to places and communities to more itinerant and scattered spaces of belonging; from being steeped in radical theory to forms of knowledge arising through lived experience; from being well known in radical circles to being known primarily among friends, loved ones, and close collaborators.

Some we interviewed in person, some over conference calls, and others through written correspondence. We have tried to show this conversation—and to keep it going—by including extended excerpts from some of the interviews, putting them in dialogue with our own ideas and with each other. Some people we interviewed were unequivocally enthusiastic about this notion of joyful militancy, offering encouragement and affirmation. Others were more critical, alerting us to dangers, shortcomings, and confusion, and challenging some of our ideas. We have tried to show some of the ways our interlocutors challenged and disagreed with us—and diverged from each other—without pitting anyone against each other in a simplistic way.

We learned a lot from the apprehensiveness of some of the Indigenous people and people of color we interviewed, whose emotions are constantly policed and regulated, and whose struggles are constantly appropriated or erased. We heard from them that centering things like kindness, love, trust, and flourishing—especially when it comes from white people like us—can erase power relations. It can end up pathologizing so-called "negative" emotions like fear, mistrust, resentment, and anger. It can legitimize tone policing and a reactionary defense of comfort. It can fall into simplistic commandments to "be nice" or "get over" oppression and violence. Similarly, pointing to the importance of trust and openness can be dangerous and irresponsible in a world of so much betrayal and violence. These misgivings have taught us to be clear that trust and vulnerability are powerful *and* irreducibly risky; they require boundaries. They can never be obligations or duties.

We have also found that Spinoza's concept of sadness can be very misleading. In contrast to joy, it means the *reduction* of one's capacities to affect and be affected. Initially we had been calling rigid radicalism "sad militancy," drawing on others in the Spinozan current.[8] But while the concept of sad militancy was immediately intuitive for some, for others it was frustrating because of its resonance with grief and sorrow, which are an irreducible part of life and struggle. Interpreted in this light, it could be seen as belittling grief and pain. For that reason, we have decentered the concept of sadness in this book, while trying to hang onto what Spinoza was getting at. In its place, we often use words like stagnation, rigidity, and depletion, connoting a loss of collective power and the way Empire and rigid radicalism keep us stuck there. With joyful militancy we are trying to get at a multiplicity of transformations and worlds in motion, but there is a danger of implying that we are all in the same situation, and erasing difference and antagonisms. BIPOC women, trans, queer, and Two-Spirit people, in particular, have worked hard to show the specificities of the oppression they face *and* the specificity of their resistance and the worlds they are making.

In the face of this, we have mostly questions and tentative ideas: Can joyful militancy affirm and explore a multiplicity of struggles and forms of life without homogenizing them? By attuning us to open-endedness of situations, can joy help us undo some of the universalizing and colonizing tendencies of radical Western theory and practice? Can movements be explored in ways that enable mutual learning and transformation rather than erasing difference?

Here we want to return to the dynamic space beyond fixed norms on the one hand, and "anything goes" relativism on the other. Outside this false dichotomy is the domain of relationships that are alive, responsive, and make people capable of new things together, *without* imposing this on everyone else. It is in this space where values like openness, curiosity, trust, and responsibility can really flourish, not as fixed ways of being to be applied everywhere but as ways of relating that can only be kept alive by cultivating careful, selective, and fierce boundaries. For joy to flourish, it needs sharp edges.

How do we know when to be open and vulnerable and when to draw lines in the sand and fight? Who to trust, and how? When are relationships worth fighting for, and when do they need to be abandoned? These are not questions with pre-given answers; they can only be answered over and over again in a multiplicity of ways. A crucial outgrowth of joy and fidelity to it, we suggest, is that people will take different paths and have different priorities. Movements and forms of life will diverge and sometimes come into conflict. There is no trump card that can be used to dictate a path to others: not the state, not morality, and not strategic imperatives of unity or movement-building. Encountering difference might lead to new capacities, strong bonds, and new forms of struggle. Or it might be more ambivalent and difficult, mixing distance and closeness. Or it might mean being told to fuck off. For all these reasons, we try to share some of our own values, and some of the struggles and movements that deeply inspire us, without saying that they are right for everyone or that others should share our priorities.

STRUCTURE OF THE BOOK

This book is laid out in five core chapters. Each chapter looks at Empire from a different perspective, showing how it is being undone at the edges and cracks. Chapter 1 suggests that increasingly Empire works through subjection and the accumulation of powerlessness. Backed by violence, its promises of happiness work like an anesthetic, closing subjects off from transformation. Joy is the growth of an embodied thinking and doing that undoes this stifling subjection.

In chapter 2 we look at how Empire maintains its hold through morality and toxic relationships. As an alternative to the false choice between duty-bound moralism or isolated individualism, we recover a conception of relational ethics from the Spinozan current. In conversation with others, we use this relational ethics to think through the potentials and pitfalls of alliances across the settler colonial divide and other forms of oppression, suggesting that Empire's hold is undone by selective openness, fierce boundaries, and new and old forms of kinship and friendship.

We deepen this relational ethics in chapter 3, arguing that joyful militancy is sustained by emergent values—common notions—of trust and responsibility. We suggest that these capacities have been stolen from us by forced dependence on Empire's infrastructures and institutions, which monopolize the ways we live and die together. Drawing on stories from transformative justice, youth liberation, and Indigenous resurgence, we look at some of the ways people are able to undo this dependence and figure things out together.

Chapters 4 and 5 track the ways that Empire has seeped into radical movements and spaces. Attempts to root out Empire have paradoxically fueled some of its most debilitating tendencies, including suspicion, moralism, rigidity, and shame, turning radical politics into a competitive performance rather than a shared and enabling process. In chapter 5 we tell three tangled stories about the historical emergence of rigid radicalism, looking at the way ideology has permeated Marxism, anarchism, and other movements; how schooling has promoted a paranoid search for flaws and limitations; and how moralism crops up in radical spaces, leading to guilt, shame, and puritanism. In each of these stories, we try to show how rigid radicalism is constantly being undone and warded off by other ways of being, ethical responsiveness, strong relationships, and common notions.

Ultimately we want joyful militancy to be about questions and curiosity, not fixed answers or instructions. In this spirit we hope that this book contributes to ongoing conversations and that it supports people in figuring out for themselves what thriving resistance looks like and how rigidity and stagnation can be warded off.

Chapter 1: Empire, Militancy, and Joy

A concept is a brick. It can be used to build a court-
house of reason. Or it can be thrown through the
window.

—Brian Massumi[1]

Personally, I want to be nurturing life when I go down
in struggle. I want nurturing life to BE my struggle.

—Zainab Amadahy[2]

Resistance and joy are everywhere

Anyone who has been transformed through a struggle
can attest to its power to open up more capacities for
resistance, creativity, action, and vision. This sense of

collective power—the sense that things are different, that *we* are different, that a more capable "we" is forming that didn't exist before—is what we mean by joyful transformation. Joyful transformation entails a new conception of militancy, which is already emerging in many movements today. To be militant about joy means being attuned to situations or relationships and learning how to participate in and support the transformation rather than directing or controlling it.

Everywhere people are recovering, sustaining, and re-inventing worlds that are more intense and alive than the form of life offered up by Empire. The web of control that exploits and administers life—ranging from the most brutal forms of domination to the subtlest inculcation of anxiety and isolation—is what we call Empire. It includes the interlocking systems of settler colonialism, white supremacy, the state, capitalism, ableism, ageism, and heteropatriarchy. Using one word to encapsulate all of this is risky because it can end up turning Empire into a static thing, when in fact it is a complex set of processes. These processes separate people from their power, their creativity, and their ability to connect with each other and their worlds.

We say *worlds*, in the plural, because part of Empire's power is to bring us all into the same world, with one morality, one history, and one direction, and to convert differences into hierarchical, violent divisions. As other worlds emerge through resistance and transformation, they reveal more of the violence of Empire. Insurrections and revolts on the street reveal that the police are an armed gang and that "keeping the peace" is war by other means. Pushing back against sexualized violence reveals the ways that rape culture continues to structure daily life. Indigenous resurgence reveals the persistent concreteness of settler colonial occupation and the charade of apologizing for genocide and dispossession as if they were only part of the past. Holding assemblies where people can formulate problems together, make decisions collectively, and care for one another reveals the profound alienation and individualism of life under Empire. Trying to raise kids (or even share space with them) without controlling them reveals the ways that ageism and schooling stifle young people and segregate generations. Struggles against anti-Black racism and white supremacy reveal the continuities between slavery, apartheid, and mass incarceration, in which slave catchers have evolved into police and plantations have shaped prisons. The movements of migrants reveal the interconnected violence of borders, imperialism, and citizenship. And the constant resistance to capitalism, even when fleeting, reveals the subordination, humiliation, and exploitation required by capital. As these struggles connect and resonate, Empire's precarity is being revealed everywhere, even if it continues to be pervasive and devastating.

There is no doubt that we live in a world of intertwined horrors. Borders tighten around bodies as capital flows ever more freely; corporations suck lakes dry to sell bottled water; debt proliferates as a tool of control and dispossession; governments and corporations attack Indigenous lands and bodies while announcing state-controlled recognition and reconciliation initiatives; surveillance is increasingly ubiquitous; addiction, depression, and anxiety proliferate along with new drugs to keep bodies working; gentrification tears apart neighborhoods to make way for glassy condos; people remain tethered to jobs they hate; the whole world is becoming toxic; bombs are dropped by drones controlled by soldiers at a distant computer console; a coded discourse of criminality constructs Black bodies as threats, targeting them with murder and imprisonment; climatic and ecological catastrophes intensify as world leaders debate emissions targets; more of us depend on food and gadgets made half a world away under brutal conditions; we are encouraged to spend more time touching our screens than the people we love; it is easier for many of us to envision the end of the world than the end of capitalism.[3]

We suspect that anyone reading this already knows and feels this horror in one way or another. When we say that struggles *reveal* the violence of Empire, it's not that everyone was unaware of it before. However, upwellings of resistance and insurrection make this knowing *palpable* in ways that compel responses. In this sense, it is not that people first figure out how oppression works, then are able to organize or resist. Rather it is resistance, struggle, and lived transformation that make it possible to feel collective power and carve out new paths.

Sadness and subjection

No, the masses were not innocent dupes; at a certain point, under a certain set of conditions, they wanted

fascism, and it is this perversion of the desire of the
masses that needs to be accounted for.

—Deleuze and Guattari[4]

In order to rule, those in positions of power need to constantly crush and subdue the forces of transformation. They
do not merely need obedience; they need their subjects to
be separated from their own capacities. As Audre Lorde
writes, "Every oppression must corrupt or distort those various sources of power within the culture of the oppressed
that can provide energy for change."[5] Empire's hold is increasingly *affective:* it suffuses our emotions, relationships,
and desires, propagating feelings of shame, impotence, fear,
and dependence. It makes capitalist relations feel inevitable
and (to some) even desirable.

An important insight shared by many radical currents
is that these forms of violence and control are ultimately toxic for everyone. For men to "enjoy" the benefits of
patriarchal masculinity, their capacities for vulnerability
and care must be eviscerated, replaced by a violent and
disconnected way of being built upon shame and wound-
edness. For white people to become white, they have to
internalize entitlement and a hostility to difference, hid-
ing from the ways their lives depend on institutionalized
violence and exploitation. Settlers must build their lives
on a living legacy of genocide, indebted to ongoing extraction and dispossession. Being privileged by Empire means
being sheltered from its most extreme forms of violence
and degradation, and to be enrolled in a stultifying form

of life that re-creates this violence. Most of what is called privilege has nothing to do with thriving or joy; this is why privileged white men are some of the most emotionally stunted, closed-off people alive today. None of this is to deny that there are pleasures, wealth, and safety associated with whiteness, heteropatriarchal masculinity, and other forms of privilege. Instead, it is to insist that everyone, potentially, has a stake in undoing privileges—and the ongoing violence required to secure them—as a part of transformative struggle. As Jack Halberstam writes in his introduction to Fred Moten's *The Undercommons,*

> The mission then for the denizens of the under-commons is to recognize that when you seek to make things better, you are not just doing it for the Other, you must also be doing it for yourself. While men may think they are being "sensitive" by turning to feminism, while white people may think they are being right on by opposing racism, no one will really be able to embrace the mission of tearing "this shit down" until they realize that the structures they oppose are not only bad for some of us, they are bad for all of us. Gender hier-archies are bad for men as well as women and they are really bad for the rest of us. Racial hierarchies are not rational and ordered, they are chaotic and nonsensical and must be opposed by precisely all those who benefit in any way from them. Or, as Moten puts it: "The coalition emerges out of your recognition that it's fucked up for you, in the same

way that we've already recognized that it's fucked
up for us. I don't need your help. I just need you
to recognize that this shit is killing you, too, however much more softly, you stupid motherfucker,
you know?"[6]

Empire is killing all of us, in different ways, and all of
us, in different ways, are marked by incredible legacies of
movement and revolt. Its forms of control are never total,
never guaranteed. The word "sabotage" comes from those
who destroyed factory machinery by throwing their wood-
en shoes (*sabots*) in the gears of the early European factories. Slaves broke their tools in the field, poisoned their
masters, learned to read in secret, and invented subversive
forms of song and dance.

Empire reacts to resistance by entrenching and accumulating what Spinoza called *sadness*: the reduction of
our capacity to affect and be affected. We've chosen not
to use this word very much in this book because we've
found it can be misleading in many ways, but the concept
of sadness is important for Spinoza. In the same way that
joy gets conflated with happiness, it's easy to hear "sad" in
terms of its familiar meaning as an emotion rather than
the way Spinoza intended it: as a reduction of capacities. For Spinoza, sadness cannot be avoided or eliminated
completely; it is part of life. All things wax, wane, and die
eventually, and the process can provoke thought, resistance,
and action. Sadness and joy can be intertwined in complex
ways. But Empire *accumulates* and *spreads* sadness. Drawing
on Spinoza, here is how Deleuze put it:

> We live in a world which is generally disagreeable, where not only people but the established powers have a stake in transmitting sad affects to us. Sadness, sad affects, are all those which reduce our power to act. The established powers need our sadness to make us slaves. The tyrant, the priest, the captors of souls need to persuade us that life is hard and a burden. The powers that be need to repress us no less than to make us anxious ... to administer and organize our intimate little fears.[7]

Empire propagates and transmits sad affects. Sadness sticks to us; we are made to desire its rhythms. Terrible situations are made to feel inevitable. For this reason, we speak of the entrenchment of Spinozan sadness as that which is stultifying, depleting, disempowering, individualizing, and isolating. But this entrenchment might not feel agonizing or even unpleasant: it might feel like comfort, boredom, or safety. We have found the notion of "subjection" helpful here, because it goes beyond a top-down notion of power. In an interview, the critical trans scholar and organizer Dean Spade explains why he uses this term instead of the more common activist term "oppression":

> "Subjection" suggests a more complex set of relationships, where we are constituted as subjects by these systems, engage in resistance within these systems, manage and are managed within these systems, and can have moments of seeing and exploiting the cracks and edges of these systems. I chose

to introduce this term, despite its unfamiliarity in most activist realms I am part of, because I felt its intervention was a necessary part of my argument about how power works.[8]

Today, especially in the metropolitan centers of so-called "developed" countries, subjects are enmeshed in a dense fabric of control. Some of us are steered into forms of life that are compatible and complicit with ongoing exploitation and violence, while other populations are selected for slow death. New forms of subjection are invented to contain each new rebellion, enrolling subjects to participate in the containment. Prisons and policing come to be felt (especially by white people) as a form of safety and security. Misogyny is eroticized, and objectification reaches new heights, taking new forms. Desires for affluence and luxury are entrenched amid growing inequality. Through cellphones and social media, surveillance and control are increasingly participatory. When they are working, these forms of subjection are felt not as impositions but as *desires*, like a warm embrace or an insistent tug.

Joy is not happiness

With all this in mind, we want to pull happiness and joy apart, in hopes of further clarifying what we mean by joyful militancy. The happiness offered to us by Empire is not the same as joy, even though they are conventionally understood as synonyms. For instance, the *Oxford English*

Dictionary defines joy simply as "a feeling of great pleasure or happiness."[9] But whereas joyful transformation undoes the stultifying effects of Empire, happiness has become a tool of subjection.

Under Empire, happiness is seen as a duty and unhappiness as a disorder. Marketing firms increasingly sell happy experiences instead of products: happiness is a relaxing vacation on the beach, an intense night at the bar, a satisfying drink on a hot day, or the contentment and security of retirement. As consumers, we are encouraged to become connoisseurs and customizers, with an ever more refined sense of the kinds of consumption that make us happy. As workers, we are expected to find happiness in our job. Neoliberal capitalism encourages its subjects to base their lives on this search for happiness, promising pleasure, bliss, fulfillment, arousal, exhilaration, or contentment, depending on your tastes and proclivities (and your budget).

The search for happiness doesn't just come through consumption. Empire also sells the *rejection* of upward mobility and consumerism as another form of placid containment: the individual realizes that what *really* makes one happy is a life in a small town where everyone knows your name, or a humble nuclear family, or kinky polyamory, or travel, or witty banter, or cooking fancy food, or awesome dance parties. The point is not that these activities are wrong or bad. Many people use food, dance, sex, intimacy, and travel in ways intertwined with transformative struggles and bonds. But Empire empties these and other activities of their transformative potential, inviting us to shape our lives in pursuit of happiness as the ultimate goal of life. Rebecca Solnit explains this powerfully:

> Happiness is a sort of ridiculous thing we're all sup-
> posed to chase like dogs chasing cars that suggests
> there's some sort of steady wellbeing ... you can feel
> confident, you can feel loved, but I think joy flashes
> up at moments and then you have other important
> things to attend to. Happiness—the wall-to-wall
> carpeting of the psyche—is somewhat overrated.[10]

Similarly, feminist theorist Sara Ahmed writes that "to be conditioned by happiness is to like your condition ... consensus is produced through sharing happy objects, creating a blanket whose warmth covers over the potential of the body to be affected otherwise."[11] As wall-to-wall carpeting or a warm blanket, the search for happiness closes off other possibilities, other textures, other affections. Ahmed shows how the promise of happiness can be treacherous, encouraging us to ignore or turn away from suffering—our own or others'—if it threatens happiness. This promise has a gendered and racialized logic: Empire is designed to secure white male happiness in particular, while the feelings of women, genderqueer and trans folks, and people of color are intensely policed. As Nishnaabeg scholar and artist Leanne Betasamosake Simpson writes,

> I am repeatedly told that I cannot be angry if I
> want transformative change—that the expression of
> anger and rage as emotions are wrong, misguided,

and counter-productive to the movement. The un-
derlying message in such statements is that we, as
Indigenous and Black peoples, are not allowed to
express a full range of human emotions. We are encouraged to suppress responses that are not deemed
palatable or respectable to settler society. But the
correct emotional response to violence targeting
our families is rage.[12]

Simpson shows how the restriction of negative emotions can take place in movements themselves: imperatives
to be happy, nice, or kind can sustain violence, forcing out
anger and antagonism. Unhappiness is pathologized along
with so-called "negative" emotions like rage, despair, resentment, and fear when they get in the way of promised forms
of happiness.

For those who refuse these imperatives, control and
coercion lurk behind happy promises. Being perceived as a
threat to the happiness of others—especially white men—
can be lethal. These tangled webs of subjection are portrayed as individual failings or pathologies. Unhappiness,
outrage, and grief are then perceived as individual disor-
ders, to be dealt with through pharmaceuticals, self-help,
therapy, and other atomizing responses.

The point is not that happiness is always bad, or
that being happy means being complicit with Empire.
Happiness can also be subversive and dangerous, as part
of a process through which one becomes more alive and
capable. But when happiness becomes something to be
gripped or chased after as the meaning of life, it tends to

lose its transformative potential. And if we are not happy—if we are depressed, anxious, addicted, or "crazy"—we are tasked with fixing ourselves, or at least with managing our symptoms. The wall-to-wall carpeting of happiness is an *anaesthetic* under Empire.

The challenge is not to reject happiness in favor of duty or self-sacrifice but to initiate processes of thinking, feeling, and acting that undo subjection, starting from everyday life. Because Empire has shaped our very aspirations, moods, and identities, this always entails grappling with parts of ourselves. This is one of the fundamental questions that runs through the Spinozan current: How are people made to desire their own stifling forms of subjection? How do we come to desire the violent, depleting forms of life offered up by Empire? How do transformative movements get drawn back into the rhythms of capitalism and the state? And, most importantly, how can we bring about something different?

Because Empire has a hold on our desires and the rhythms of our lives, undoing it cannot be about discovering a truth or revealing it to others as if we have all been duped. The kind of transformation we are interested in is not about converting people or finally being able to see clearly.

The power of joy

To emphasize joy, in contrast to happiness, is to move away from conditioned habits, reactions, and emotions. Bubbling up in the cracks of Empire, joy remakes people through combat with forces of subjection. Joy is a *desubjectifying* process, an unfixing, an intensification of life itself.[13] It is a process of coming alive and coming apart. Whereas happiness is used as a numbing anesthetic that induces dependence, joy is the growth of people's capacity to do and feel new things, in ways that can break this dependence. It is *aesthetic*, in its older meaning, before thinking and feeling were separate: the increase in our capacity to perceive with our senses. As Mexican activist and writer Gustavo Esteva explained in his interview with us,

> We use the word "aesthetic" to allude to the ideal of beauty. The etymological meaning, almost lost, associates the word with the intensity of sensual experience; it means perceptive, sharp in the senses. That meaning is retained in words like anaesthesia. Comparing a funeral in a modern, middle-class family and in a village in Mexico or India, we can see then the contrast in how one expresses or not their feelings and how joy and sadness can be combined with great intensity.[14]

Esteva suggested to us that *sentipensar* still carries this meaning in Spanish: the conviction that you cannot think without feeling or feel without thinking. As the feminist scholar Silvia Federici explained when we interviewed her, joy is a palpable sense of collective power:

> I like the distinction between happiness and joy. I like joy, like you, because I think joy is an active

passion. It's not a stagnant state of being. It's not satisfaction with things as they are. It's part of feeling power's capacities growing in you and growing in the people around you. It's a feeling, a passion, that comes from a process of transformation. And it's a process of growth. So this doesn't necessarily mean that you have to be satisfied with your situation. It means that again, using Spinoza, that you understand the situation, and you're active in a way that you feel that you are comprehending and moving along in accordance to what is required in that moment. So you feel that you have the power to change and you feel yourself changing with what you're doing, together with other people. It's not a form of acquiescence to what exists.[15]

This feeling of the power to change one's life and circumstances is at the core of collective resistance, insurrections, and the construction of alternatives to life under Empire. Joy is the *sentipensar*, the thinking-feeling that arises from becoming capable of *more,* and often this entails feeling many emotions at once. It is resonant with what the Black poet and intellectual Audre Lorde calls the erotic:

> For once we begin to feel deeply all the aspects of our lives, we begin to demand from ourselves and from our life-pursuits that they feel in accordance with that joy which we know ourselves to be capable of. Our erotic knowledge empowers us, becomes a lens through which we scrutinize all

aspects of our existence, forcing us to evaluate those
aspects honestly in terms of their relative meaning
within our lives. And this is a grave responsibility,
projected from within each of us, not to settle for
the convenient, the shoddy, the conventionally expected, nor the merely safe.[16]

Lorde makes it clear that this capacity for feeling is not
about fleeting pleasure or contentment: following its line
requires responsibility and pulls one away from comfort
and safety. It undoes stuckness. It makes stultifying com-
forts intolerable. In our interview with writer and activist adrienne maree brown, she emphasized that joy is the
capacity to be more fully present with ourselves and the
world:

I feel very fortunate that my mother read *The
Prophet* by Khalil Gibran to me many times. There
is this whole thing on how your sorrow carves
out the space for your joy, and vice versa. That has
helped me a lot. In recent years I have been on a
path to learn somatics, how to be in my whole-
ness, with my trauma, with my triggers, with my
brilliance. It's all about being present, being awake
inside your real life in real time.[17]

In this sense, joy does not come about by avoiding
pain, but by struggling *amid and through it*. To make space
for collective feelings of rage, grief, or loneliness can be
deeply transformative. Empire, in contrast, works to keep

its subjects stuck in individualizing sadness: held in habits and relationships that are depleting, toxic, and privatized. This stagnation might be held in place by the pursuit of happiness and the attempt to numb or avoid pain. To be more fully present, in contrast, means tuning in to that which affects us and participating actively in the forces that shape us.

This tuning-in might be subtle and tender, or it might be a violent act of refusal. Sometimes these shifts are barely perceptible and take place over decades, and sometimes they are dramatic and world-shaking. For Deleuze, thought begins from cramped spaces where one is hemmed in by the forces of subjection. It is not an act of individual will but a scream that interrupts unbearable forces, opening space for more active combat.[18] This is why so many movements and struggles begin with a scream of refusal: NO, ¡Ya Basta!, Enough!, Fuck off. They interrupt Empire's powers of subjection and make new practices and new worlds possible. One spark of refusal can lead to an upwelling of collective rage and insurrection. In this way, joy can erupt from despair, rage, hopelessness, resentment, or other so-called "negative" emotions.

Similarly, in a nihilistic vein, the anonymous authors of the queer journal *Bædan* unpack *jouissance* as something that exceeds simple enjoyment or pleasure, conceiving it as an ecstatic rupture in the social order imposed by Empire:

> We should analyze this distinction between plea-
> sure and pain as being an inscription of the social
> order into our bodies. And in the same way, it is

the mundane and miniscule pleasures produced through contemporary power arrangements which keep us dependent on those arrangements for our well-being. *Jouissance*, in abolishing both sides of this distinction, severs us from pain as a self-preservation instinct and from pleasure as the society's alluring bribe. It is the process that momentarily sets us free from our fear of death (literal or figurative) which is such a powerful inhibitor.

We can locate this *jouissance* in the historic moments of queer riot: Compton's cafeteria, Dewey's, the White Night, Stonewall, and countless other moments where queer bodies participated in rupture—throwing bricks, setting fires, smashing windows, rejoicing in the streets. But more to the point, *jouissance* is located in precisely the aspects of these moments (and of others unknown to us) which elude historians, the ones which cannot be captured in a textbook or situated neatly within narratives of progress for queer people, or of rational political struggle for a better future.[19]

Jouissance is difficult to pin down because it is movement and transformation itself. By breaking the divide between pleasure and pain, it undoes habits that hold subjects in place. We are not suggesting that there is some hidden unity behind queer nihilist *jouissance*, the notion of the erotic in Black feminism, or the Latin American concept of *sentipensar*. But we do think that these and other currents resonate with the Spinozan concept of joy: a process that is transformative, dangerous, painful, and powerful but also somewhat elusive. A paradox of joy is that it can't be described fully; it is always embodied differently, as different struggles open up more space for people to change and be changed. In fact, to grip it, to nail it down, to claim to represent it fully would be to turn it into a dead image divorced from its lively unfolding. The way to participate in joyful transformation is through immersion in it, which is impossible if one is always standing back, evaluating, or attempting to control things.

Another part of why joyful transformation is difficult to talk about is because of the inheritance of a dualistic, patriarchal worldview in which "real" change is supposed to be measurable and observable, and "intelligence" is the capacity for a detached engineering of outcomes. Even the capacity to live otherwise and reject parts of Empire is often presented in patriarchal ways: the subject of revolution is the heroic, strong-willed individual who has the capacity to see past illusions and free himself from mistakes and errors of the past. As feminist, queer, anti-racist, and Indigenous writers have pointed out, this is a vision that falls back on the detached, masculine individual as the basic unit of life and freedom.

Rather than trying to rationally direct the course of events, an affective politics is about learning to participate more actively in the forces that compose the world and oneself. This is what Spinoza meant by intelligence. Supporting joy cannot be achieved through a detached rationality but only through attunement to relationships, feelings, and forces—a practical wisdom that supports flourishing and experimentation.[20] This is how organizer and militant researcher Marina Sitrin put it when we spoke with her:

> I am so excited for this project. It all resonates deeply with things I have been thinking, witnessing, fearing, and dreaming. The role of joy, in particular in the way you describe it, is often absent—though not entirely—from our conversations and constructions in the northern part of the Americas and Europe. It is both a fairly large and abstract concept, and at the same time a very simple, direct, and emotive one. How do we feel when we participate in a movement or group? What are our relationships to others in the group? Does it feel open? Caring? Social? Is there trust? Why do we come back to assemblies and actions? Are people open to one another?[21]

These questions are not just about whether people feel good. They are about how spaces and struggles affect us, and about the potential of becoming more alive, open, trusting and creative. Practices that seem to resemble each other might be vastly different, in terms of what they enable affectively (or don't). Depending on the context, the relationships, and the way things unfold, a tactic like a strike or a street demo might be based on a dismal conformity to habit or duty, or it might be a profound experience that connects people in new ways and opens possibilities for creativity and movement. It might also be a messy mix of stale routines, reactive containment, and transformative potential.

As we explore in the next chapter, transformative power might look like a dramatic break from the relationships and life paths that have been offered by Empire, but it might also involve more subtle work of learning to love places, families, friends, and parts of ourselves in new ways. It entails deepening some bonds while severing others, and enabling selective openness through firm boundaries. What could it mean to be militant or fiercely committed to all this? Is it possible to be militant about creativity and care? Can militancy be something that is responsive and relationship-based? Can people be militant about joy?

Militant about joy

We want to connect joy to militancy for a number of reasons. We are interested in how the capacity for refusal and the willingness to fight can be enabling, relational, and open up potentials for collective struggle and movement, in ways that are *not* necessarily associated with control, duty, or vanguardism. We want an expansive conception of militancy that affirms the potential of transformation at the expense of comfort, safety, or predictability. A common definition of militancy is to be "vigorously active, combative and aggressive, especially in support of a cause."[22] We are interested in the ways that putting joy into contact with militancy helps link fierce struggle with intense affect: rebellions and movements are not only about determined resistance but also about opening up collective capacities. With joyful militancy we want to get at what it means to enliven struggle *and* care, combativeness *and* tenderness, hand in hand.

However, the historical associations and current renderings of militancy are complex. Historically, militancy is often associated with Marxist-Leninist and Maoist vanguardism and the ways these ideologies have informed revolutionary class struggle and national liberation struggles. These ideals of militancy have been challenged, especially by Black, Indigenous, and postcolonial feminists, who have pointed out the pitfalls of rigid ideology, patriarchal leadership, and the neglect of care and love. The traditional figure of the militant—zealous, rigid, and ruthless—has also been challenged by situationism, anarchism, feminism, queer politics, and other currents that have connected direct action and struggle to the liberation of desire, foregrounding the importance of creativity and experimentation. From this perspective, the militant is the one who is always trying to control things, to take charge, to educate, to radicalize, and so on. This kind of militant tends to be two steps behind transformations as they manifest themselves, always finding them lacking the correct analysis or strategy, always imposing a framework or program.

The contemporary discourse of counterterrorism associates figures of militancy with ISIL, the Taliban, and other groups named as enemies of the United States and its allies.[23] In this way, the specter of the "militant extremist" helps justify further militarization, surveillance, imperialism, and Islamophobia. The suspected presence of one militant is enough to turn a whole area into a strike zone in which all military-aged men are conceived as enemy combatants and everyone else as collateral damage. Within this discourse, the militant is increasingly the ultimate Other, to be targeted for death or indefinite detention. In all of these representations—from the Maoist rebel to the terrorist extremist—the figure of the militant tends to be associated with intense discipline, duty, and armed struggle, and these ways of being are often posed in opposition to being supple, responsive, or sensitive. It's clear that militancy means willingness to fight, but in its dominant representations it is cold and calculating.

At the same time, there are other currents of militancy that make space for transformation and joy. When we interviewed her, queer Filipino organizer Melanie Matining spoke about its potential to break down stereotypes:

> The word "militancy" for me is a really, really hard one. It was used a lot in Filipino organizing. I would always connect it to the military industrial complex, and I didn't want to replicate that. And then as I started peeling back the actual things we need to do.... As an Asian woman, to be militant— that's really fucking rad. It breaks down sterotypes of submissiveness. The concept of militancy is a new thing for me, and to embrace it I'm unpacking notions of who I'm supposed to be.[24]

Artist and writer Jackie Wang argues that militancy is not only tactically necessary but also transformative for those who embody it. In the context of anti-Blackness in the United States, Wang shows how the category of

"crime" has been constructed around Blackness and how
mass incarceration has led to a politics of safety and re-
spectability that relies on claims of innocence, contrasted
implicitly with (Black) guilt and criminality. Rejecting
the politics of innocence means challenging the innocent/
criminal dichotomy and the institutionalized violence
that subtends it. This form of militancy, Wang argues,
is "not about assuming a certain theoretical posture or
adopting a certain perspective—it is a lived position."[25]
Drawing on Frantz Fanon, Wang writes that militancy
has the capacity "to transform people and 'fundamentally alter' their being by emboldening them, removing
their passivity and cleansing them of the 'core of despair'
crystallized in their bodies."[26] Living militancy, from this
perspective, is inherently connected to a process of transformation that undoes the knot of subjection around innocence, challenges the carceral logics of anti-Blackness,
and opens up new terrains of struggle.

When we asked Indigenous political theorist Glen
Coulthard about his conception of militancy in the context of Indigenous resurgence, he called it an "emergent
radicalism" that destabilizes relations of domination.[27]
Coulthard's work focuses on Indigenous resurgence and
resistance to settler colonialism. He reveals the ways
that Empire represents Indigenous peoples' oppression
as a constellation of personal failings and "issues" to be
addressed through colonial recognition and reconciliation. He also focuses on Indigenous refusal and resistance, the revaluation of Indigenous traditions, and a rise
in Indigenous militancy and direct action. Militancy, in

the context of Indigenous resurgence, is about the capacity to break down colonial structures of control, including the state's monopoly on the legitimate use of force; it is a break with the colonial state's attempt to subjugate Indigenous people and ensure continued exploitation of Indigenous lands. This emergent militancy isn't based on a single program or ideology but comes out of relationships. As Coulthard says:

> It's emergent in the sense that it's bottom-up. But it also emerges from something… those relationships to land, place, community. So that is the emergent part. Emergent doesn't mean entirely new, because those relationships to place are not new. They've always been there and are always re-emerging. It comes in cycles. The always-there emergent militancy is acted on through management strategies, recognition and accommodation, whatever. That has its effects: it dampens the crisis; it overcomes contradictions temporarily. And then the militancy will emerge again. And we've seen this four or five times in the last half-century, these series of containment/management strategies…
>
> What's always prior is agency of Indigenous peoples, and capital and the state are constantly on the defensive, reacting. As opposed to thinking that we're always reacting to colonialism when we privilege it. It's this resurgent Indigenous subjectivity that the state is constantly trying to quell or subdue. And it's successful but never totally successful. And

it boils over, comes to the surface, and some new technology is deployed in order to manage it, and reconciliation is the latest tool that is doing that work. But it's always because of our persistent presence: we've never gone away, and we've been articulating alternatives in words and deeds.[28]

This conception of militancy as emergent is important because it doesn't come out of thin air or from an enlightened vanguard of militarized men who suppose that they can see things more clearly than common people. It comes out of the ongoing refusal of Indigenous peoples to give up their ways of life. As Kiera Ladner and Leanne Betasamosake Simpson write in their introduction to *This Is an Honour Song*,

> The summer of 1990 brought some strong medicine to Turtle Island. For many Canadians, "Oka" was the first time they encountered Indigenous anger, resistance and standoff, and the resistance was quickly dubbed both the "Oka Crisis" and the "Oka Crises" by the mainstream media. But to the Kanien'kehaka (Mohawk) people of Kanehsatà:ke, who were living up to their responsibilities to take care of their lands, this was neither a "crisis" at Oka, nor was it about the non-Native town of "Oka." This was about 400 years of colonial injustice. Similarly, for the Kanien'kehaka from Kahnawà:ke and Akwesasne who created "crises" by putting up their own barricades on the Mercier Bridge or by

mobilizing and/or mobilizing support (resources) at Kanehsatà:ke, this really had nothing to do with Oka, a bridge or a golf course. This was about 400 years of resistance. Like every Indigenous nation occupied by Canada, the Haudenosaunee have been confronting state/settler societies and their governments since those societies began threatening the sovereignty, self-determination, and jurisdiction of the Haudenosaunee. It was not a beginning. Nor was this the end. This was a culmination of many, many years of Onhkwehonwe resistance resulting in a decision to put up barricades in defense of, and to bring attention to, Haudenosaunee land ethics, treaty responsibilities, and governance.[29]

Indigenous resurgence and events like Oka are not joyful in the sense of being happy but in the sense that they are deeply transformative and able to catalyze solidarity across Turtle Island. But unlike Marxist conceptions of militancy in which the vanguard is supposed to usher in a global revolution, it is clear that Indigenous struggles do not implicate everyone in the same way. As it breaks down colonial structures of control and dispossession, Indigenous resurgence implicates us, as settlers, in complicated ways: it unsettles us and our relationship to land and place, and it throws into question received ideas about who we are, our responsibilities and complicities, what it means to live here, and our received ideas about what "here" is. It compels us to learn, together, how to support Indigenous resurgence and resist settler colonial violence.

Joyful militancy has also emerged in spaces where people generate the capacity to move *with* despair and hopelessness, to politicize it. In her study of the queer movement ACT UP, queer theorist and activist Deborah Gould shows how its militant tactics not only won institutional victories that prolonged and saved lives; it was also a process of world-making:

> From its start and throughout its life, ACT UP was a place to fight the AIDS crisis, and it was always more than that as well. It was a place to elaborate critiques of the status quo, to imagine alternative worlds, to express anger, to defy authority, to form sexual and other intimacies, to practice non-hierarchical governance and self-determination, to argue with one another, to refashion identities, to experience new feelings, to be changed.[30]

The militancy of ACT UP was not only about a willingness to be confrontational and defy conventions of straight society and mainstream gay and lesbian politics; the movement also created erotically charged queer atmospheres and sustained networks of care and support for members who got sick. Catalyzed by grief and rage, it blew open political horizons and changed what was possible for people to think, do, and feel together.

When we asked the Argentina-based intellectual Sebastián Touza about militancy, he discussed the danger of defining it once and for all:

I don't know if militancy can be defined as such. Probably it is not a good idea to define it that way because that would entail a general point of view, an interchangeable and abstract concept, valid for all situations. But, on the other hand, I would say that a militant is somebody who struggles for justice in the situation.... Thus we have to pay attention to the situation, to the encounters that take place in it, to how meaning is elaborated there, to the subjectivities that arise as a result of those encounters.[31]

This "situated" militancy does not start from a prefabricated notion of justice. It is an attempt to intervene effectively in the here and now, based on a capacity to be attuned to relationships. An example of this could be Touza's discussion of the struggle of the Mothers of Plaza de Mayo, a feminist organization that formed in resistance to military repression in Argentina in the 1970s:

Mothers grew up not from strategic plans but from below: from the pain of mothers seeking to recover their children who had been kidnapped, tortured, and "disappeared" by the state. Because they have not separated affects from political activity, Mothers never consider each other means toward ends. Nobody has to be subordinated to strengthen the organization. Rather, they regard each other as ends in themselves. What bonds them together is not an idea but the affect, love and friendship that arises from supporting each other, sharing intimate emotions, moments of joy and sorrow. They organize themselves through consensus, understood not as a system of decision-making or conflict resolution but as a direct engagement with the lives of one another. As in a now long established feminist tradition, for them the personal is political. Mothers guide themselves by an ethics of intimate conviction whose exercise cannot be detached from everyday life. They have a profound distrust of ideologies and party lines and are proud of their autonomy from the state, political parties, unions, and NGOs. Their autonomy does not consist in fighting against a dominant ideology, which might summon the need for the specialized knowledge of a vanguard party, but rather ... in the affirmation of liberating aspects of popular culture that already exist among them.[32]

The Mothers are a powerful example of how militancy often springs from everyday life and the bonds of kinship rather than abstract ideological or moral commitments. These struggles eventually waned or were absorbed by Empire, at least partially. The Argentinean government eventually began using the discourse of human rights and began to offer money and services as an attempt to relegitimize the state and regain control, causing deep divisions between the Mothers and other movements in Argentina.[33] The Canadian government used treaty negotiations, reconciliation discourses, and other formal processes in an attempt to quell Indigenous resurgence and militancy. As Coulthard explains above, new forms of militancy tend to provoke new strategies of containment and absorption by the state, leading to the invention of new forms of struggle. None of these movements stayed frozen in one form: in various ways they transformed, dissolved, shifted, or were institutionalized. But the fact that Empire always invents new forms of containment is not evidence that movements have failed or that they were misguided. Joyful transformation sometimes ebbs and flows, becomes captured or crushed, grows subtler or percolates into everyday life, but always re-emerges and renews itself.

Militancy is not a fixed ideal to approximate. We cannot be "like" a militant because militancy—in the way we conceptualize it here—is a practice that is based in the specificity of situations. We cannot become these examples, nor should we look to them as ideals. Rather than boiling joyful militancy down to a fixed way of being or a set of characteristics, we see it arising in and through the relationships that people have with each other. This means it will always look different, based on the emergent connections, relationships, and convictions that animate it.

In relation to this, we believe it is important to hesitate, lest our understanding of militancy become another form of rigid radicalism. Not everyone we spoke with has been enthusiastic about this word. For instance, in our interview with them, writer and artist Margaret Killjoy was ambivalent, emphasizing its connection to armed struggle:

> I guess I see it as being someone who is "actively"
> involved in trying to promote radical social change
> and in a non-reformist way. It's dangerous as termi-
> nology ... I don't use it much myself ... because of
> course the first implication it seems to have is that
> of armed struggle, which is far from a universally
> applicable strategy or tactic.[34]

We hope that joyful militancy allows for questions and
uncertainties that are too often smothered by conventional
conceptions of militancy. We also recognize that many will
still prefer different language. We are not suggesting that
all joyful struggles share an ideology, a program, or a set of
tactics. What the above examples have in common is that
they express a form of militancy that is attuned to their local situations and arises from people's needs, desires, and
relationships. What we are calling joyful militancy is not a
shared content, though we do think there are some shared
values and sensibilities. Rather it is an attunement and activation of collective power that looks different everywhere,
because everywhere *is* different.

Besides these highly visible examples, joyful militancy
also lives in art and poetry that opens people's capacities for
thinking and feeling in new ways. It is expressed in quiet
forms of subversion and sabotage, as well as all the forms of
care, connection, and support that defy the isolation and
violence of Empire. It is not a question of being a certain
way but a question of open-ended becoming, starting from
wherever people find themselves.

Starting from where people find themselves

Joy arises not from the pursuit of a distant goal but through struggle in one's own situation. It often erupts through the capacity to say no, to refuse, or to attack the debilitating form of life offered up by Empire. It might come through a riot or a barricade. Or it might come about by refusing Empire's offers of insipid happiness or through the capacity to be present with grief. Ultimately it is up to people to figure this out for themselves by composing gestures, histories, relationships, feelings, textures, world events, neighborhoods, ancestors, languages, tools, and bodies in a way that enables something new, deepening a crack in Empire. This is at odds with the stiff, macho militancy that attempts to control change from above. It cannot be a kind of more-radical-than-you stance that occupies a fixed position or argues for a single way forward.

How do we create situations where we feel more alive and capable than before? What makes the intransigence of oppression feel a little less stable? What might create more room to move and breathe? What supports people to refuse the all-too-common traps of moralism, clarity, or perfectionism in favor of increasing collective power and creativity? The answers to these questions are infinitely varied and complex. Being militant about collective, enabling transformation is about trust in people's capacities to figure out this way forward together, along with a willingness to participate openly in the process.

Chapter 2: Friendship, Freedom, Ethics, Affinity

To become what we need to each other, and to find power in friendship, is to become dangerous.

—anonymous[1]

I have a circle of friends and family with whom I am radically vulnerable and trust deeply—we call it co-evolution through friendship.

—adrienne maree brown[2]

The urgency of making kin[3]

Empire works in part by constantly attenuating and poisoning relationships. Kinship has been enclosed within the nuclear family, freedom within the individual, and values within morality. Together these enclosures sap relationships of their intensity and their transformative potential. If relationships are what compose the world and our lives, then the "free individual" of modern, Western capitalism (an implicitly straight, white, able-bodied, cis-gendered, property-owning man) is a sad and lonely vision: a strange fiction invented by a violent and fearful society, walled in by morality and self-interest. This is an uprooted being who sees his rootlessness—his very incapacity to make and sustain transformative connections—as a feat of excellence.

We suggest that Empire's grip on relationships is being broken by new and resurgent forms of intimacy through which people come to depend on each other, defend each other, and become dangerous together. Friendship as freedom, in this story, names interdependent relationships as a source of collective power, a dangerous closeness that Empire works to eradicate through relentless violence, division, competition, management, and incitements to see ourselves as isolated individuals or nuclear family units.

Spinoza helps us dissolve the fiction of the modern Western individual—and its oscillation between self-interest and morality—into a relational *ethics*. A lot of people already navigate their everyday lives in this way, attuned and responsive to their own situations and relationships. Along these lines, we draw on a minor current of anarchism associated with Gustav Landauer and others that centers relationships as the basis of resistance and movement. We bring these currents into conversation with Indigenous worldviews and practices, along with the ethical questions that are being asked and answered in a multiplicity of ways, in different places, around decolonizing relationships between settlers and Indigenous people. This conversation always includes questions of how to sever harmful relationships. Freedom, in this sense, is not just the capacity to generate "good" relationships, but also to draw lines in the sand and fight.

Friendship is the root of freedom

> These are not just words; they are clues and prods
> to earthquakes in kin making that are not limited to
> Western family apparatuses, heteronormative or not.
> —Donna Haraway[4]

Freedom and friendship used to mean the same thing: intimate, interdependent relationships and the commitment to face the world together. At its root, relational freedom isn't about being unrestricted: it might mean the capacity for interconnectedness and attachment. Or mutual support and care. Or shared gratitude and openness to an uncertain world. Or a new capacity to fight alongside others. But this is not what freedom has come to mean under Empire.

Look for the dictionary definition of "freedom" today and you'll find *rights, absences* and *lack of restrictions* at the core, applied to an isolated individual. Here are some of its definitions in the *Oxford English Dictionary*:

The power or right to act, speak, or think as one wants:

"we do have some freedom of choice"

The state of not being imprisoned or enslaved:

"the shark thrashed its way to freedom"

The state of not being subject to or affected by (something undesirable):

"government policies to achieve freedom from want"[5]

At bottom, all of these definitions are about getting away from external restriction or influence: being unhindered, unaffected, independent. Under capitalism, freedom is especially associated with free markets and the free agent who chooses based on individual preferences. In spite of colonization and capitalism, this vapid form of freedom still can't get a foothold in many parts of the world. Even in Europe, where so many tools of colonization were refined, the roots of freedom were different. Centuries ago, some Europeans had a more relational conception of freedom, which wasn't just about the absence of external constraints, but also about our immersion in the relationships that sustain us and make us thrive.

"Freedom" and "friend" share the same early Indo-European root: **fri-*, or **pri-*, meaning "love."[6] This root made its way into Gothic, Norse, Celtic, Hindi, Russian, and German.[7] A thousand years ago, the Germanic word for "friend" was the present participle of the verb *freon*, "to love." This language also had an adjective, **frija-*. It meant "free" as in "not in slavery," where the reason to avoid slavery was to be among loved ones. *Frija* meant "beloved, belonging to the circle of one's beloved friends and family."[8] As the Invisible Committee writes in *To Our Friends,*

> "Friend" and "free" in English … come from the same Indo-European root, which conveys the idea of a shared power that grows. Being free and having ties was one and the same thing. I am free because I have ties, because I am linked to a reality greater than me."[9]

A few centuries later, freedom became untied from connectedness. The seventeenth-century philosopher Thomas Hobbes imagined freedom as nothing more than an "absence of opposition" possessed by isolated, selfish individuals. For Hobbes, the free man is constantly armed and on guard: "When going to sleep, he locks his doors; when even in his house he locks his chests."[10] The free individual lives in fear and can only feel secure when he knows there are laws and police to protect him and his possessions. He is definitely *he,* because this individual is also founded on patriarchal male supremacy and its associated divisions of mind/body, aggression/submission, rationality/emotion, and so on. His so-called autonomy is inseparable from his exploitation of others.

When peasants were "freed," during this period, it often meant that they had been forced from their lands and their means of subsistence, leaving them "free" to sell their labor for a wage in the factories or starve. It is no coincidence that these lonely conceptions of freedom arose at the same time as the European witch trials, the enclosure of common lands, the rise of the transatlantic slave trade, and the colonization and genocide of the Americas. At the same time as the meaning of freedom was divorced from friendship and connection, the lived connections between people and places were being dismembered.

As Empire was enclosing lands and bodies, it was overseeing the enclosure of thought as well. The Age of Reason was marked by a new kind of knowledge that could subdue and control nature and the human body, enabling capitalist rationalization and work discipline.[11] Time and space would become measurable, stable, and fixed. Bodies were no longer conduits for magical forces but machines to be harnessed for production. Plants, animals, and other nonhuman creatures were no longer kin but objects to be dissected and consumed.

Even among intellectuals in Europe, not everyone agreed with Hobbes's fearful vision of freedom and the divisions imposed by Cartesian thought. Descartes's contemporary, Baruch Spinoza, articulated a philosophy in which people were inherently intertwined with their world. Spinoza left instructions for his most important work, the *Ethics,* to be published after his death, because he knew he would likely face torture and execution for the ways his relational worldview undermined both monotheistic religion and the dualistic philosophy that was emerging during his own time. Instead of a passive Nature on one hand and an active, supernatural God on the other, Spinoza envisioned a holistic reality in which God is present in all things, and in which all things are active and dynamic processes. Everything is alive and connected. Mind and body, human and nonhuman, joy and sadness, are intertwined with one another.

We do not mean to present Spinoza's philosophy as a handbook for living in today's world. In many ways, Spinoza remained a product of his time and place: he used the geometric method to create proofs for his philosophical claims, he couldn't overcome patriarchal divisions, and he remained wedded to the state as a vehicle for security. Our interest is not in Spinoza himself, or even his philosophy as a whole, but in the way that his ideas are part of a minor current in Western thought that is more relational, holistic, and dynamic. Spinoza's work remains marginal compared to that of Descartes and Hobbes, but his relational worldview has nevertheless been taken up by radicals at the margins of philosophy, ecology, feminism, Marxism, and anarchism.[12]

Most importantly, for us, Spinoza's philosophy is grounded in affect.[13] Things are not defined by what they are but by what they *do:* how they affect and are affected by the forces of the world. In this way, capabilities are not fixed for all time but are constantly shifting. This is a fundamental departure from the inherently ableist and ageist perspective that measures all bodies in relation to the norm of a "healthy," "mature," or "able" body. When starting right from a body's material specificity, without any intervening "should," learning becomes fundamentally different: rather than detached categorization or observation of stable properties, it happens through active experimentation in shared, ever-changing situations.

From morality to ethics

By creating a philosophy based in affect, Spinoza initiated a radical critique of ruling institutions and authorities and the ways they exercise control through subjection, including toxic morality inherited from centuries of Christianity, heteropatriarchy, capitalism, and the state. But Spinoza's philosophy did not just undermine Empire's dominant morality in order to replace it with a different one; it undermined *morality itself.* His worldview was at odds with any notion of an ultimate ground of right and wrong that was uniform for everyone, abstracted from the lively flux of relationships and situations. For Spinoza, life was an exploration of the forces of the world, not conformity to a fixed ideal.

For moralists this is dangerous because there's no guarantee against evil, and no ultimate foundation for moral judgment. Yet the Spinozan lineage is not about everyone doing whatever they please, according to isolated interests and preferences. On the contrary, recognizing our interconnectedness means becoming capable of *more* fidelity to our web of relations and our situations, not less. This fidelity is not moral; it is *ethical*.

Ethics is often spoken of colloquially as an individual morality: a static set of principles held by individuals (ethical consumption, codes of ethics, and so on). In fact, dictionary definitions conflate ethics with the "moral principles that govern a person's behavior."[14] But as Deleuze explains, a Spinozan conception of ethics results in a completely different set of questions:

> There's a fundamental difference between Ethics and Morality. Spinoza doesn't make up a morality, for a very simple reason: he never asks what we must do, he always asks what we are capable of, what's in our power, ethics is a problem of power, never a problem of duty. In this sense Spinoza is profoundly immoral. Regarding the moral problem, good and evil, he has a happy nature because he doesn't even comprehend what this means. What he comprehends are good encounters, bad encounters, increases and diminutions of power. Thus he makes an ethics and not at all a morality.[15]

Whereas morality asks and answers the question: "what should one do?" a Spinozan ethics asks: "what is one capable of?" Unlike the cold abstraction of morality, a body's capacities can only be discovered through attunement and experimentation, starting right where you are. You never know until you try. In trying, whether you "succeed" or "fail," you will have learned and changed, and the situation will have changed, even if only slightly. This sounds simple, and in many ways it is. It speaks to the ways that many of us already try to navigate our everyday lives: not by adhering to fixed commandments but by learning to inhabit our own situations in ways that make us more capable and more jointly alive.

Someone gets in touch with bird migrations, insects, weather patterns: they affect her more and more deeply as she tunes into their rhythms, over months and years. They begin to make her up. The loss is palpable as fewer return each year, and her hatred of the destruction grows alongside her love of the few remaining refuges for nonhuman creatures where she lives. Her rage and despair finds resonance with others, similarly entwined, and they figure out how to fight together. This is neither individual self-interest nor moral altruism. It is relational ethics: the willingness to nurture and defend relationships.[16]

Two friends fold their lives together; they draw new capacities out of each other. They hurt each other, and they work through it, emerging more intertwined than before. They are no longer sure which ideas and mannerisms were "their own" and which belonged to the friend. They know each other's triggers and tendencies intimately. One finds himself in trouble, and the other drops everything to help, at great personal risk. But this risk and sacrifice is not because it is morally right or because they have calculated that it is in their own self-interest. It is not even felt as a choice; it is something drawn out of them.

Ethics is the dynamic space beyond static morality and vapid self-interest: it is the capacity to be responsive to the relationships that make us up. Whether consciously or not, our desires and choices are the product of everything that affects us. While this kind of thinking and practice may be intuitive, it runs against dominant strands of both Western knowledge and morality, which strive for universalism and generalizability: they tend towards pinning things down, dictating how we should act, or predicting what is likely. They ask what humans are and always will be, what we should always do, or what we usually do (and how we can be controlled). In contrast, a Spinozan ethics is attuned to the singularity and openness of each situation: what are we capable of here and now, together, at *this* time, in *this* place, amid the relations in which we are embedded?

From this perspective, it is not about creating self-contained units but about participating in complex, shifting, relational processes. We always begin in the middle: amid our situations, in our neighborhoods, with our own penchants, habits, loves, complicities, and connections. There is no individual that comes before the dense network of relations in which we're embedded. This relational space eludes the traps of individual self-interest *and* moral duty. It is a space beyond isolated individuals and altruistic saviors. We are always participating in the making of our worlds and being made by them. From this perspective, freedom can mean nothing other than the ethical expansion of what we're capable of—what we're able to feel and do together. In this vein, the Invisible Committee writes,

> Freedom isn't the act of shedding our attachments, but the practical capacity to work on them, to move around in their space, to form or dissolve

them ... the freedom to uproot oneself has always been a fantasmic freedom. We can't rid ourselves of what binds us without at the same time losing the very thing to which our forces would be applied.[17]

Freedom here is not the absence of restriction or attachment but the capacity to become more active in shaping our attachments. This becoming-active is not about controlling things but about learning to participate in their flow, forming intense bonds through which we become implicated in each other's struggles and capacities. Within the Spinozan current, friendship is being revalued: not as a bond between individuals but as an ethical relation that remakes us, together, in an ongoing process of becoming otherwise. Similarly, feminist philosopher Donna Haraway has argued that "making kin" across divides of species, nation, gender, and other borders is perhaps the most urgent task today.[18] Through friendship or kinship we undo ourselves and become new, in potentially radical and dangerous ways. In this sense, friendship is at the root of freedom.

What can friendship do?

Friendship will be the soil from which a new politics will emerge.

—Ivan Illich[19]

Can friendship be revalued as a radical, transformative form of kinship? We are not sure, but we want to try. Maybe the concept of friendship is already too colonized by liberalism and capitalism. Under neoliberalism, friendship is a banal affair of private preferences: we hang out, we share hobbies, we make small talk. We become friends with those who are already like us, and we keep each other comfortable rather than becoming different and more capable together. The algorithms of Facebook and other social networks guide us towards the refinement of our profiles, reducing friendship to the click of a button.[20] This neoliberal friend is the alternative to hetero- and homonormative coupling: "just friends" implies a much weaker and insignificant bond than a lover could ever be. Under neoliberal friendship, we don't have each other's backs, and our lives aren't tangled up together. But these insipid tendencies do not mean that friendships are pointless, only that friendship is a terrain of struggle. Empire works to usher its subjects into flimsy relationships where nothing is at stake and to infuse intimacy with violence and domination. Perhaps friendship can be revalued in an expansive but specific way: friends, chosen family, and other kin intimately connected in a web of mutual support.

Intersecting currents of disability justice, youth liberation, queer movements, feminism, ecology, anarchism, Indigenous resurgence, and Black liberation have all emphasized the centrality of nurturing strong relationships. In our conversation with Glen Coulthard, he emphasized that joyful militancy can never be an individual choice because transformation happens in and through relationships:

The first move toward some sort of self-affirmation or resurgence is often registered in a very negative reaction: hate, envy, these sorts of things.... This complicates the story a bit. In order to have a kind of joyful militant positionality or whatever, it requires a whole lot of other overwhelming positions on the world. And that is where I think relationships are crucial. I don't think that this is even possible to come to on your own. Am I going to respond to this oppressive situation through a form of self-destruction, or am I going to try and live with it, or am I going to channel it into more community-building efforts? And I don't think that's ever done in a silo. Those are comrades that are working together in order to achieve that position. Those are through the hard conversations ranging from interventions to who-knows-what, just recognizing that some relationships seem to be more empowering than others. So getting to be the joyful militant is complicated. It's a product of relationships. It's not the effect of doing relationships well; it's because we're already in relationships of solidarity. We're helping each other out, we're drawing people out of the negative into more positive relationships. Joyful militants aren't choosing and saying "oh, I'm going to do this."

It's because I'm being interpellated into more positive relationships, which provide me with different perspectives on the world, that draw me away from what would be entirely acceptable

and rational, and that's despair. How do we not
have despair in these situations that we're in? It's
because relationships are drawing us away from
that to the extent that they can, to the extent
that they're successful. A joyful militant is less a
product of a will to do so; there's a work, we're
constantly working on each other. I'm not gonna
blame the individual person if they're in a situation
that is clearly miserable.[21]

In these times, feelings of despair, rage, and hatred
make sense. Maybe they even indicate a healthy receptivity
to what is taking place, a refusal to numb ourselves to the
pain and violence of Empire. To shame people for being in
touch with all this, or to tell them to pull themselves out
of it, simply individualizes suffering. Change comes not
from individuals but from this "constant working on each
other," which we have called ethics and relational freedom.
It might entail supporting each other to become more present with despair, guilt, resentment, fear, or grief. It might
include channeling anger into attacking Empire, blocking
its flows, or breaking its hold, at least in part. Freedom is
the space that opens when knee-jerk reactions and stifling
habits are suspended. It is the parents learning to trust their
kid. It is the teen who flees a violent home with support
from friends. It is the scream of refusal that elicits rage and
action from others. But the key is that one never does any
of this alone, whether a humble gesture causing a subtle
shift or a decisive act catalyzing dramatic change. Freedom,
gentleness, and militancy always come from—and feed

back into—the web of relationships and affections in which everyone is immersed.

By creating relational webs that reinforce the values we aspire to, relationships can help undo patterns that Empire has ingrained. Loving relationships can be what allow us to face the things we fear about ourselves. They can help undo the ways that we have internalized notions that we are not good enough, not worthy of love, or that we have to put up with things that deplete us and those we care about. Relationships of mutual love and support can enable us to see and feel the toxicity of some of our attachments. They can help us to look at our patterns of addiction or depression without shame. Those we love can be our reasons to stay alive when we aren't sure that we want to. They can help us leave miserable situations by leaping with us into the unknown. Friendships can be the source of our capacity to take risks and get in the way of violence and exploitation. They can be what make us dangerous and capable of fighting in new ways. This might be something like what "friend" meant to some of our European ancestors before the witch trials: not just someone to hang out with, but also someone whose existence is inseparable from one's own. A relationship crucial to life, worth fighting for.

A persnickety linguist or historian might object that there is no unbroken line of insurgent friendship that lies hidden in history. These critics are right: it is a zigzagging, disjointed line, always being broken and reassembled, a story among other stories, resonant with many other non-European genealogies of relational freedom. But this elusiveness is what makes it precious and powerful: it is people's capacity to constantly form new complicities amid terror and violence.

Solidarity begins at home

> I don't need to be empowered by adults; I need them to stop having power over me.
>
> —Lilah Joy Bergman, age 9

While friendship is made vapid by Empire, coupledom and the nuclear family become the container for all other forms of intimacy. As anti-racist, Indigenous, and autonomist feminists have shown, the nuclear family—where one generation of parents lives with one generation of children, separated from everyone else—is a recent invention of Empire.[22] It was (and is) a crucial institution for the privatization and enclosure of life. It is also central to the maintenance of a culture of authoritarianism, abuse, and neglect that underpins heteropatriarchy and white supremacy. It evolved as a way of reproducing wage-laboring men through the unpaid labor of women. Violence against women and children within the family was condoned as part of a civilizing process, and it became a conduit for intergenerational violence and for the accumulation of white wealth and property through inheritance.

Through feminist struggle, some of the most brutal, state-sanctioned violence of the nuclear family (such as legalized rape and abuse) have been challenged, but it remains a site of isolation and violence, for children in particular. One of its most brutal effects is that it makes other forms of intimacy difficult or unthinkable for many of us. Through suburbs and apartments designed for a privatized existence, the nuclear family is even coded into the built environment.

At the same time, people are constantly inventing and recovering other kinds of belonging and intimacy. They are creatively collectivizing and communalizing life, sharing income, food, and housing in ways that break down privatization and segregation. As Silvia Federici writes,

> We also have a return to more extended types of families, built not on blood ties but on friendship relations. This, I think, is a model to follow. We are obviously in a period of transition and a great deal of experimentation, but opening up the family— hetero or gay—to a broader community, breaking down the walls that increasingly isolated it and prevented it from confronting its problems in a collective way is the path we must take not to be suffocated by it, and instead strengthen our resistance to exploitation. The denuclearisation of the family is the path to the construction of communities of resistance.[23]

Many Indigenous people, people of color, and queer folks have never been invited into the structure of the nuclear family, and they have always made kin in other ways. Queer chosen families have created intimate, intergenerational webs of support, and these radical ties remain alive in spite of new forms of homonormative capture. As Dean Spade writes,

> In the queer communities I'm in valuing friendship is a really big deal, often coming out of the fact that lots of us don't have family support, and build deep supportive structures with other queers. We are interested in resisting the heteronormative family structure in which people are expected to form a dyad, marry, have kids, and get all their needs met within that family structure. A lot of us see that as unhealthy, as a new technology of post-industrial late capitalism that is connected to alienating people from community and training them to think in terms of individuality, to value the smaller unit of the nuclear family rather than the extended family.[24]

Similarly, bell hooks points to traditions of informal adoption in Black communities, in which people adopted and cared for children in ways that were communally recognized but never sanctioned by the state:

> Let's say you didn't have any children and your neighbor had eight kids. You might negotiate with her to adopt a child, who would then come live with you, but there would never be any kind of formal adoption, yet everybody would recognize her as your "play daughter." My community was

unusual in that gay black men were also able to informally adopt children. And in this case there was
a kinship structure in the community where people
would go home and visit their folks if they wanted
to, stay with them (or what have you), but they
would also be able to stay with the person who was
loving and parenting them.[25]

Leanne Simpson, writing on Indigenous nationhood,
notes how resurgence entails displacing settler colonialism and the nuclear family with "big, beautiful, diverse,
extended multiracial families of relatives and friends that
care very deeply for each other."[26] In many ways, these kinds
of relationships make possible and sustain the creation of
intergenerational forms of organizing that include kids and
elders and break down divides between public and private.
Simpson spoke to the importance of this when we interviewed her:

How change happens matters to me, which is why I
don't spend much time lobbying the state. I believe
in creating the change on the ground, and creating
and living the alternatives. In my nation, children
and Elders are critical, and it means we organize
differently. You can't invite kids to a twelve-hour,
boring meeting and then get frustrated because
they are bored or frustrated because they won't stay
with the childcare worker they've never met. You
can't invite the Elders to welcome people to the territory and then not speak to the issues. I think we

actually need to do less organizing and more movement building. Right now, we have activists, not
leaders. We have actions, not community. My kids
are also fundamentally not interested in "the movement." They are, however, fundamentally interested
in doing things.[27]

These kinds of non-nuclear kinship networks have
been sustained in the face of state terrorism and incarceration, residential and boarding schools, and Empire's ongoing attempts to privatize and destroy non-nuclear kinship
networks, extended families, and webs of relationships
that include nonhuman kin. Nourishing and sustaining
these communal forms of life throws into question some
of the dominant ideas about what counts as political work,
about separation of activism or organizing from everyday
life. They challenge the segregation of kids from the rest of
the world (and from organizing and politics in particular)
and the ways that elders are isolated and intergenerational
connections are lost.

Creating intergenerational webs of intimacy and
support is a radical act in a world that has privatized
child-rearing, housing, subsistence, and decision making.
Challenging the nuclear family is not about a puritanical
rejection of anything that resembles it; it is about creating alternatives to its hegemony, to the dismembering of
social relations, to the spatial division of people through
suburbanization, incarceration, schooling, dispossession, and displacement. This entails the proliferation of
relationships that may or may not be based on blood but

are built on care and love. The Latin American political theorist Raúl Zibechi argues that non-nuclear family and kinship networks are at the heart of Latin America's most transformative and militant movements, including those of Indigenous peoples, peasant farmers, landless and homeless movements, *piqueteros*, and women's and youth movements.[28] These collective forms of life are based in new forms of dwelling, subsistence, and resistance. At the same time, Zibechi is clear that these are "only tendencies, aspirations, or attempts in the midst of social struggles."[29] Relationships of mutual support are not a destination but a continual process of struggle.

As people renew intergenerational relationships and bring their whole lives into struggle, new forms of politics emerge. In this context, Silvia Federici argues,

> This is why the idea of creating "self-reproducing" movements has been so powerful. It means creating a certain social fabric and forms of co-operative reproduction that can give continuity and strength to our struggles, and a more solid base to our solidarity. We need to create forms of life in which political activism is not separated from the task of our daily reproduction, so that relations of trust and commitment can develop that today remain on the horizon. We need to put our lives in common with the lives of other people to have movements that are solid and do not rise up and then dissipate. Sharing reproduction, this is what began to happen within the Occupy

Movement and what usually happens when a struggle reaches a moment of almost insurrectional power. For example, when a strike goes on for several months, people begin to put their lives in common because they have to mobilise all their resources not to be defeated.[30]

Federici here gets at the way in which care is not only a means of maintaining struggles but also a transformative part of struggle itself. While Empire works to privatize and individualize our daily lives, many movements are reproducing themselves more autonomously by collectivizing care: from cooking to cohabitation to learning to just being present with each other.

Friendship, kinship, and communalization have also been at the heart of working across the hierarchical divides of heteropatriarchy, white supremacy, colonization, ableism, ecocide, and other systems that have taught us to enact violence on each other and internalize oppressive ways of relating. To make kin across these divisions is a precarious and radical act. Everyone knows how difficult this can be and how people fuck up, hurt each other, and blame each other. Those conscripted into oppressive roles can always fall back into old habits. In some cases, people are able to talk about all this in ways that are subtle, gentle, and more attuned to each other's tendencies, triggers, and gifts, and genuine relations of support emerge. In the context of queer, anti-racist disability justice, Mia Mingus speaks to the centrality of strong relationships for undoing oppression:

Any kind of systematic change we want to make will require us to work together to do it. And we have to have relationships strong enough to hold us as we go up against something as powerful as the state, the medical industrial complex, the prison system, the gender binary system, the church, immigration system, the war machine, global capitalism.

Because we're going to mess up. Of that I am sure. We cannot, on the one hand have sharp analysis about how pervasive systems of oppression and violence are and then on the other hand, expect people to act like that's not the world we exist in. Of course there are times we are going to do and say oppressive things, of course we are going to hurt each other, of course we are going to be violent, collude in violence or accept violence as normal.

We must roll up our sleeves and start doing the hard work of learning how to work through conflict, pain and hurt as if our lives depended on it— because they do.[31]

Between the authors of this book, friendship has required us to negotiate divisions ingrained in our bodies by ageism, patriarchy, capitalism, and ableism. Sometimes these divisions get in the way of our capacity to connect in ways that are enabling and transformative. Patriarchy has socialized Nick, as a man, to be self-assured, (over)confident, rational, and individualistic. carla has been socialized to be submissive, caring, diffident, and to put others before herself. Even as we worked against some of these tendencies, carla ended up doing more emotional and caring labor for this project and Nick ended up doing more labor when it came to writing and editing. We have also been learning to challenge these divisions, always partially and inconsistently, through processes of mutual growth, support, and (un)learning. In part because of our very different life experiences, skill sets, and perspectives, our collaborative process has enabled us to produce something new together and made us both more capable in new ways. Neither of us could have written this book, or anything like it, alone.

The ethics of affinity in anarchism

Ultimately, nourishing these kinds of intimacies means putting relationships before abstract political commitments and ideologies. At the same time, we think it is possible to recover relational currents within anti-authoritarian political traditions without appropriating the ideas and struggles of others. Within anarchism, the Spinozan current flows through Gustav Landauer's relational conception of anarchism. Landauer's philosophy ran against the grain of the dominant strands of revolutionary Marxism and anarchism of his time, which conceived revolution as a dramatic event that would take place in the future. Instead of envisioning a future event of transformation in which capitalism and the state would be destroyed and all of humanity could be liberated, Landauer insisted on the importance of a *living, present* anarchism and on transforming our relationships here and now.

Landauer also argued that the state's power lies not
only with armies or police but also in its capacity to get us
to govern ourselves and each other and to re-create its hierarchical and divisive relationships through our conduct:

> A table can be overturned and a window can be
> smashed. However, those who believe that the state
> is also a thing or a fetish that can be overturned or
> smashed are sophists and believers in the Word.
> The state is a social relationship; a certain way of
> people relating to one another. It can be destroyed
> by creating new social relationships; i.e., by people
> relating to one another differently.[32]

The state and capitalism are systems designed to amass
wealth for a tiny minority, and while Empire's figureheads
are people with names and addresses, others will replace
them when they are gone. Instead of destroying Empire,
Landauer raised the question of how to undo its hold on relationships and how to generate new and different relations
in its place. This is an ethical question, not a moral one.
Like Spinoza, he suggested that that there was no single answer for everyone. He insisted that a notion of worldwide
socialism or anarchism was too totalizing, and he recognized that other people and cultures would have different
answers to the question of how to live:

> We have long enough misunderstood socialism as
> a vague, general ideology, a magic wand that opens
> all doors and solves all problems. We should know

> by now that everything out in the world as well
> as within our souls is so jumbled that there will
> never be only one way to happiness. So what I am
> advocating here has nothing to do with a call on
> humanity. We have to realize that different cultures
> exist next to each other and that the dream that all
> should be the same cannot be sustained – in fact, it
> is not even a beautiful dream.[33]

In a way that resonates with many anti-authoritarian currents of today, Landauer refused to hold anarchism up as a single moral or ideological project that would free all of humanity from oppression. But while refusing this universalizing project, Landauer was also critical of individualist anarchists like Max Stirner, who also refused morality but rooted his philosophy in the liberation of the individual ego or desire.[34] In contrast, Landauer insisted that individual people could not be abstracted from their already existing relationships, values, and communities. Like the state, the self-enclosed individual is a fiction of Empire. "I" am already a crowd, enmeshed in others.

For Landauer, then, transformation was an *immediate, situated, ethical project* that could only be based on transforming ourselves, collectively, starting from where we are and seeking out affinities with others. "Only when anarchy becomes, for us, a dark, deep dream, not a vision attainable through concepts," Landauer wrote, "can our ethics and our actions become one."[35] Similarly, scott crow writes, "Anarchism is not rigid, it is flexible and fluid so cast aside your thoughts about the way it 'should' be and help make it what it 'could be.'"[36] Freedom, in this sense, is not the absence of Empire, secured through a glorious future revolution or the triumph of an anarchist blueprint. Freedom is the capacity to grapple with some of the toxic habits and relationships fostered by Empire and to recover other ways of relating. This anarchism can only be an action or a process.

Anarchist political theorist Richard Day has drawn on Landauer, Kropotkin, and others to reveal a current of anarchism that is about the capacity to create immediate, living alternatives to the state, capitalism, morality, and Empire's oppressive divisions. There are always forms of alliance and mutual aid that exceed Empire, from the ways plants and animals support each other symbiotically to everyday forms of cooperation and solidarity that crop up in spite of subjection. Day calls this the *logic of affinity*, which is "ever-present, even in the most advanced forms of (post)industrial bureaucratic control. It is not a dream, but an actuality; not something to be yearned for, but something to be noticed in operation everywhere, at every moment of every day."[37] From this perspective, affinity can be discerned in every process of joyful transformation, large and small, in which people discover new capacities together, resist, invent, or activate something that is already in play. The capacity to carve out autonomous forms of life is always under attack by Empire and always resurfacing.

This concept of affinity is important to us because it gets at the way forms of life can connect based in shared commitments or desires *without* erasing differences. We follow Day in suggesting that there is an "affinity for affinity" among currents of Indigenous, anti-racist, anti-colonial, migrant justice, anarchist, feminist, ecological, queer, and autonomist currents of thought and practice: a penchant for linking up and supporting others based on shared values and commitments without trampling on each other's autonomy.[38] It can be seen, for example, in the Zapatistas' vision of "a world where many worlds fit."[39] Similarly, affinity is resonant with what Gloria Anzaldúa calls "bridging" in *This Bridge We Call Home*:

> Bridging is the work of opening the gate to the stranger, within and without. To step across the threshold is to be stripped of the illusion of safety because it moves us into unfamiliar territory and does not grant safe passage. To bridge is to attempt community, and for that we must risk being open to personal, political, and spiritual intimacy, to risk being wounded. Effective bridging comes from knowing when to close ranks to those outside our home, group, community, nation—and when to keep the gates open.[40]

These notions of affinity and bridging turn connection into an open-ended ethical question rather than an assumption, a goal, or a moral imperative. How do we relate? Who is this "we"? How do we affect each other? How and when to be open *selectively*? How might we be able to work together? These questions can only be answered by people in their own situations, as relationships unfold.

Connecting Spinozan currents to Indigenous resurgence

While we hope some of the affinities between Spinozan currents and Indigenous worldviews are emergent throughout this chapter, we want to spend some time thinking about them directly, especially in light of the relational conceptions we have outlined above. We think the relational conceptions of anarchism and friendship are resonant with (though necessarily distinct from) the lifeways of Indigenous peoples and many other societies that ground their worlds in connectedness to each other and the places they inhabit. For instance, writer and facilitator Zainab Amadahy offers a "relationship framework" that sees all life as fundamentally interconnected:

> We two-leggeds are inter-connected with each other and with other life on the planet—indeed, even to the planet itself and beyond. What we think, say, and do impacts, directly and indirectly, everything and everyone else, which also affect us. We are further impacted by ancestors and will impact generations to come. Some of us even believe the reverse; that we can impact our ancestors and that our descendants impact us. In any case, we are clearly "in relationship" whether we acknowledge, fully understand and respect the concept or not.[41]

In our conversation with Glen Coulthard, he elaborated on his notion of place-based Indigenous ethics, which he calls "grounded normativity." Coulthard shows how Indigenous resistance and values are literally *grounded* in the ongoing renewal of reciprocal relationships with land:

> I don't think you come to these things on your own. We're always kind of embedded and constituted by what's around us. The whole book I wrote [*Red Skin, White Masks*] is based on this. I'm nothing; I'm just a product of the messy relationships that have formed me over time. And the point about the book is, we've tended to think of these relationships as anthropocentric. But we're also shaped by the other-than-human relations that we're thrown into, including relationships to place and land itself, and that can have an effect on our perspective; it can shape our normativities or what we think is right or wrong.[42]

Red Skin, White Masks shows how these relational webs have been foundational for Indigenous resurgence against settler colonialism and inexorably connected to the struggle over land:

> Stated bluntly, the theory and practice of Indigenous anticolonialism, including Indigenous anticapitalism, is best understood as a struggle primarily inspired by and oriented around *the question of land*—a struggle not only *for* land in the material sense, but also deeply *informed* by what the land *as system of reciprocal relations and*

obligations can teach us about living our lives in
relation to one another and the natural world in
nondominating and nonexploitative terms.[43]

From this perspective, settler colonialism is an attack
on Indigenous bodies and lands *and* on the grounded normativities that sustain them. It is an attack on Indigenous
forms of life. For the same reason, Coulthard suggests that
recovering, sustaining, and defending these forms of life becomes crucial to decolonization and resistance:

Repetition, doing things, shapes how you see
things. And depending on what that practice is,
it can double back and shape how you do things.
And in a land-based context, that kind of cyclical,
dual conditioning, how we produce the necessities of our lives shapes our spiritual understandings, and those can, over time, double back and
shape how we go about doing things in the material sense. What we're seeing now to validate this
is that Indigenous people have been dragged away
from those practices violently, into other ones
oriented around a different mode of production,
a different way of producing the necessities of life,
through resource extraction, and that is now shaping our normative worlds, what we see as right or
wrong. And it's because these long-standing practices are being disrupted. Now what we're doing
with Dechinta and other land-based practices is
we're re-establishing—in an impure form because

we're all learning again—these different normative practices and worlds. And an important part of that is our relationship with land and other-than-human kin. So prefiguration is that emphasis on the importance of practice, and shaping even what we think our ends should be ... it's a very practical ethics.... That's not to devalue it; I actually hold this more valuable than abstract normative traditions where you have to dissociate yourself from your relationships in order to come up with pure principles, and that just results in a never-ending, always-there gap between what our ideals are and where our shitty world is at. It justifies that. In theory we have it nailed down, we just haven't quite approximated that in our lives and institutions. In contrast, the grounded normativity, practical, prefigurative starting place is saying no, those ideals are formed by what we do with our lives—by the relationships that we sustain and renew.[44]

In a way that resonates with the relational conception of anarchism we explored above, Coulthard speaks to the importance of *prefiguration*: nurturing relationships informed by reciprocity with human and other-than-human kin. Similarly, in her book *Dancing on Our Turtle's Back,* Leanne Simpson writes that she is "not so concerned with how we dismantle the master's house, that is, which set of theories we use to critique colonialism; but I am very concerned with how we (re)build our own house, or our own houses.[45]

Recovering forms of life that have been subjugated or ruled out entails resistance and transgressing of laws or norms, but these negations are only what is visible from the perspective of Empire. It is clear that this is not resistance for its own sake or (only) because Empire is monstrous: resurgent forms of life are also about values and connections worth defending and nurturing.

While there may be resonances with anarchism, Coulthard and Simpson are speaking about the resurgence of *specific, Indigenous* forms of life. Where we live, resonances and affinities between Indigenous and non-Indigenous forms of life are always marked by the violence of settler colonialism. Our lives are inextricably linked to structures bent on the eradication of Indigenous life and the exploitation of Indigenous land. Navigating these uncertain connections requires dealing with difficult ethical questions.

In our part of the world, it is clear that we are living in the midst of Indigenous resurgence. All over Turtle Island, Indigenous peoples are reasserting their ties and responsibilities to their lands, refusing the racist and heteropatriarchal divisions imposed by Empire, and recovering relationships based in care and consent. This is an intensification of what has been happening since colonization began.

For non-Indigenous people—and for white, European-descended settlers who live on Indigenous land, specifically—this can be profoundly unsettling. Can non-Indigenous people support Indigenous resurgence? Can alliances productively stretch across the colonial divide? Through messy, uneven processes, settlers and Indigenous peoples are answering these questions together. Many non-Indigenous people are beginning to see themselves *as settlers,* complicit in ongoing dispossession and colonization of Indigenous forms of life. Black and Indigenous communities are forging alliances to resist the intertwined violence of settler colonialism and anti-Blackness. As Luam Kidane and Jarrett Martineau write,

> These dreams of freedom mean that our acts of resistance are inextricably linked as Afrikan peoples and Indigenous Peoples of Turtle Island. But fundamentally, what this means is that we need to seriously, purposefully and with urgency begin to look to each other—not to the state—for our self-determination.[46]

As Indigenous resurgence and Black uprising reshape life throughout North America, new affinities and new forms of co-resistance are emerging. It is increasingly clear that decolonization is fundamental to all struggles to dismantle Empire and live differently here and now in North America. Decolonization has fundamentally shifted the values, priorities, and organizing practices of many anarchists, anti-authoritarians, and other radicals. As Harsha Walia writes,

> A growing number of social movements are recognizing that Indigenous self-determination must become the foundation for all our broader social justice mobilizing. Indigenous peoples in Canada are the most impacted by the pillage of lands, experience disproportionate poverty and homelessness,

are overrepresented in statistics of missing and mur-
dered women and are the primary targets of repres-
sive policing and prosecutions in the criminal in-
justice system. Rather than being treated as a single
issue within a laundry list of demands, Indigenous
self-determination is increasingly understood as
intertwined with struggles against racism, poverty, police violence, war and occupation, violence
against women and environmental justice.[47]

Indigenous people have forged alliances with ranch-
ers and farmers resisting pipelines, with migrants resisting
border imperialism, and with Black communities resisting
criminalization and the prison industrial complex. They
have linked up with anarchists while challenging them to
rethink colonial conceptions of nation, territory, tradition,
and authority. Some settlers are learning to take responsibility for developing relationships with the people whose
land they are on, and learning to support Indigenous leadership. Indigenous resurgence has pushed non-Indigenous
people to learn the histories and protocols of the lands
where they live, to ask what it means to honor treaties and
what it means to live on land where treaties were never
signed. In our conversation with Coulthard, he spoke to
the potential of recovering Indigenous *and* non-Indigenous
subjugated knowledge and forms of life and exploring affinities between them:

COULTHARD: If those [Indigenous] relationships to land and place
and those sustaining connections are destroyed, then our

views change on what's good, what's just. So what we're try-ing to do in terms of land-based decolonizing education is to ensure that those practical relationships that inform our philosophical systems and vice versa are maintained to the best of our ability, and that requires a struggle and conflict with the forces that are trying to destroy it.

NICK AND CARLA: It seems like white settlers are the ones who've al-lowed their own grounded normativities to be destroyed, or they have been destroyed, at least mostly. And we've been invited to participate in the destruction of Indigenous peoples' grounded normativities.

COULTHARD: I think the point that's important here is that we're talking about hegemonies. So grounded normativities are being wiped out by a hegemonic system—a system of dominance. So when you say "the problem with settler life is that it's doing this," I would say, in my more gen-erous moments, that the hegemonic settler form of life is destroying Indigenous forms of life, but settlers have a whole host of other grounded normativities that have themselves been violently ruled out of existence. Whether that's radical ecological stuff to anarchist stuff to Marxist stuff—whatever: they're subaltern knowledges and prac-tices. And there are affinities between those that we can map out and explore. There's a lot within non-Indigenous settler traditions that have suffered their own erasure that might be brought back to the fore. And that's way better than the alternative, which is stealing what we've got. So what Foucault would refer to as a resurgence of subaltern knowledges. There's a rich history of overlap and affinities that I think need to be drawn on, and are crucial to avoid the violence of cultural appropriation and "becoming Indigenous."[48]

Exploring affinities between Indigenous and non-Indigenous traditions and forms of life raises a lot of questions. There is a deep ambivalence to the recovery of non-Indigenous traditions or the creation of new alternatives, especially those that involve direct connections to land. Deepening these relationships—with seasons, territories, plants, and other-than-human forces where we live—can end up entrenching dispossession and colonization.

From conservation to farming to fishing, many settler (especially European) traditions have evolved or been sustained through Indigenous dispossession and an attack on Indigenous forms of life. Settler colonialism has always included a project of attaching white bodies to Indigenous land, and attempts to "reclaim the commons" can erase Indigenous presence.

At the same time, there are emergent alliances and relationships between settlers and Indigenous people, based in consent and shared responsibility. Settlers are critically revaluing some of their own traditions in ways that enable new affinities and solidarities. Settlers have been able to offer their own practical land-connected skills and knowledge like herbalism, bioremediation, cooking, carpentry, ecological gardening, and more, alongside the skills and knowledges held by Indigenous people.

In our experience, it has been settlers rooted in their own traditions and values who are most capable of building strong relationships with Indigenous peoples, showing up in meaningful ways, *and* decentering themselves and staying on the sidelines when it is appropriate. It is people with strong friendships—their own webs of care and support—who are able to consistently support decolonization, whether that means supporting frontline land defense struggles or urban Indigenous initiatives or cultivating meaningful, long-term relationships with local Indigenous folks where they live.

These capacities are not based on abstract morality, nor are they about having the most bang-on anticolonial analysis. They are based on a web of connectivity that enables people to think and act differently. One thing that is clear to us about Indigenous resurgence is that it is driven and sustained by these deep connections and relationships that colonization seeks to destroy. Rebuilding and sustaining these connections is clearly at the root of decolonization—for Indigenous and non-Indigenous people differently.

How can settlers and Indigenous people explore affinities between autonomous forms of life? What are the potentials and pitfalls of revitalizing non-Indigenous traditions (or inventing new ones) on stolen ground? These questions cannot be answered in the abstract but are *already being asked and answered* collectively, over and over again, in multiple ways, across different territories, movements, and struggles. Hanging on to these as ethical questions, we think, helps get beyond the shame and guilt of moralism that can be so immobilizing (and counterproductive) for settlers—especially white settlers. Instead of the narcissistic shame that impels settlers to ask for and demand absolution from Indigenous peoples, ethical questions can shift people towards active responsibility that is rooted in consent, as Indigenous people often emphasize. For us, this means finding the wiggle room of freedom—the capacity to work on our relationships—and participate in new and old forms of nurturance and resistance.

Friendship and freedom have sharp edges

> If one would have a friend, then must one also be willing to wage war for him: and in order to wage war, one must be capable of being an enemy.
> —Friedrich Nietzsche[49]

Working on relationships also means the capacity to dissolve and sever them and to block those which are harmful. Affinity and bridging require *selective* openness, with firm boundaries. In this sense, cultivating joyful militancy not only requires cultivating "good" relationships, but also severing those that are unhealthy and damaging. Coulthard drove this point home when we talked with him:

> Part of the effect that you see in joyful militancy is an attentiveness to cultivating healthy relationships. And I think that that's great; there is a productive line of flight ... but sometimes—and this is kind of what I've been thinking a lot about since writing about reconciliation and resentment—is that

the whole idea of a "good relationship"—a positive one instead of a negative one—is almost entirely co-opted by relationship-destroying structures that entrench violence, dispossession, disappearance, all these things, where we're always compelled to be productive. It's a compulsion that's insisted on and that is done asymmetrically across certain bodies. So it's a demand that's placed on us as Indigenous peoples, even in terms of having a conversation. It can even be about tone: your tone is nega-tive.... Some relationships are just bullshit, and we shouldn't be in them. We should actually draw lines in the sand more willingly, in order to avoid the kind of status quo outcome that's caused by the compulsion to always be in a positive relation-ship to others. Others might suck. We shouldn't be relating to them; we should be fighting them; we should be seeking to destroy them in some circum-stances. Because their whole identity, their whole form of life is predicated on our negation. So that's why, in Canada, Canadians can't cease to exist in the sense that they understand themselves, because it's predicated on a genocidal relationship. And there can be no mutual recognition, there can be no mutual respect, because the relationship itself negates that possibility. And that's a pretty somber situation. It's not a joyful acknowledgment.[50]

Relational freedom necessarily includes undoing de-structive relationships, dissolving or attacking depleting or harmful forces. Freedom is the capacity to make friends *and enemies*, to be open *and to have firm boundaries*. Joyful, deeply transformative relationships are only possible through vulnerability and trust, but they also entail the risk of being deeply hurt. In this context, Mia Mingus speaks to the importance of a kind of love that is assertive and accountable:

> What I'm talking about is reinventing how we love each other and knowing that solidarity is love, collaboration is love. And really, isn't that what queerness is about: loving? I am talking about growing and cultivating a deep love that starts with those closest to us and letting it permeate out. Starting with our own communities. Building strong foundations of love.
>
> And I just want to be clear, I am not talking about love that isn't accountable. I am not talking about staying in harmful and dangerous or abusive relationships. The kind of love I want us to grow is accountable and assertive. Really, I am talking about collective love, where we look out for each other.[51]

For this kind of collective love to exist, sometimes it is necessary to sever relationships. Sometimes friendship and close bonds are a messy mix of closeness, struggle, and distance. In this sense, Empire destroys our capacity to identify enemies too: morality, policing, law, and prisons are all designed to monopolize the power to decide whose actions are right and wrong, and how they should be dealt with.

For the same reason, if reduced to an imperative to always have "good relationships" with everyone and everything, joyful militancy and friendship become simplistic, reactionary, and colonial in their erasure of power relations and systemic violence. This is the hegemonic morality of Empire—the notion that Indigenous people have to "get over" the past—and it plays itself out not only in state-based efforts at "reconciliation" but also among everyday relationships between settlers and Indigenous people that reinscribe settler entitlement. Leanne Simpson spoke to this forcefully when we asked her to share her perspective on the potential of friendship between settlers and Indigenous people:

NICK AND CARLA: One of the themes that emerged in a lot of our interviews is the importance of trust and friendship for creating and sustaining joyful militancy and transformative movement infused with love. Under conditions of settler colonialism, trust and friendship between settlers and Indigenous people seems especially difficult, because settlers and our governments have violated this trust over and over, and broken trust is the status quo. What makes trust and friendship possible? Do you see it as an important part of decolonization?

LEANNE SIMPSON: My honest answer is no, I don't. Friendship has been and is used by so-called white "allies" in pretty horrible ways—everything from "my friend is native and therefore ..." to using friendship as a mechanism to protect against white guilt, to using friendship to appropriate. Friendship for me is a crazy-intimate, personal decision and it isn't helpful for me to feel pressure to trust or be friends with people I don't trust and don't want to be friends with. The white allyship takes up a lot of space and it's a lot of work for Indigenous peoples. White people love being friends with Indigenous peoples. For me, there is huge gap in our life experiences, often our interests and our politics. That doesn't mean we can't find useful and strategic ways of working together but don't make me go to potlucks or backyard BBQs and make the assumption that my personal life is part of the movement. My personal life is not for the taking.

I also see that I have a responsibility to build trust and friendships within the Indigenous community. That is important work because the forces to divide us and make us hate each other are enormous. This does indeed make our movements strong because it's community building.[52]

For us, this gets at the danger of setting up friendship or affinity as an ideal, norm, or expectation, especially across the colonial divide and other hierarchical divisions created by Empire. While Simpson speaks to the importance of building trust and friendship among Indigenous people, she is clear that settlers (particularly white settlers seeking to be allies) often end up perpetuating extractive, entitled tendencies. For settlers, getting out of the way might be more important than seeking connection.

Just as intimacy and closeness can be enabling, they can also be sources of coercion, manipulation, and exploitation. To insist on, seek out, or use friendship—and to pathologize its refusal—tends to reinforce these divisions and hierarchies rather than unravel them. It regenerates the worst of Empire, where oppressed people are expected to stay in oppressive relationships and their refusal is dismissed as "counterproductive."

Similar patterns arise to pathologize women and genderqueer folks who refuse to "get over" heteropatriarchy, Black folks and people of color who refuse to "get over" racism, and everyone else who has experienced the liberal trope of "let's all get along." Entitlement to others' time, energy, and love can be an unconscious strategy that reproduces domination through intimacy. Love and friendship can be contorted to erase power and exploitation, enforcing obedience to oppressive norms of politeness or devotion.

Joyful militancy is not a way of dividing the world into "positive" and "negative" ways of being or asking that we all get along and be happy together. Freedom always needs to retain the potential of refusal, negation, and resistance. To turn friendship into a solution or a goal is to erase the form of freedom we are getting at, which is the freedom to work at relationships—to participate more actively in the shaping of our worlds.

The active shaping of our worlds together

What makes people fight for each other, support each other in radical ways, and construct durable, loving bonds? What makes it possible for people to sever or dissolve stifling attachments or relationships? We do not think the answer is ideology; abstract political values might support short-term alliances, but we doubt their capacity to be the glue that holds people together in the long term. Instead we suggest that strong relationships are the foundation of resistance. Recovering and sustaining deeper forms of friendship and kinship are indispensable for undoing Empire's hold.

Sometimes divisions get in the way, and people hurt each other too much, too often. Sedimented habits continue to grip us, closing off potentials for being otherwise together. Maintaining transformative relationships is not easy in a world full of violence, in which Empire continually induces us (especially white, cis-male settlers) to construct flimsy relationships based in leisure and to abandon them if they are no longer pleasurable. For many who live in big cities, don't have kids, and benefit from a lot of mobility, it is always possible to go somewhere else, to find another group of people to hang out with.

We can't all be friends, and some forms of life will never be compatible. This is the ethical basis of the logic of affinity, as well: it can never be a totally inclusive, come-one-come-all process, because this would mean welcoming the worst of Empire and all of its toxic ways of relating. Some differences might mean that people cannot work together. Maybe. Differences might also signal potential for practices, orientations, and priorities that are resonant and complementary without becoming the same. Differences might then become starting points for new complicities and the growth of shared power.

If relationships are what compose the world—and what shape our desires, values, and capacities—then freedom is the capacity to participate more actively in this process of composition. Friendship and resistance are interconnected: when we are supported, we are more willing to confront that which threatens to destroy our worlds. Friendship and affinity are not things but processes and open questions, which produce partial responses, further questions, flashes of certainty and confidence, but never definitive answers.

Chapter 3: Trust and Responsibility as Common Notions

We live in capitalism. Its power seems inescapable. So did the divine right of kings. Any human power can be resisted and changed by human beings.

—Ursula K. Le Guin[1]

Do not be afraid
Do not be cynical
Continue to trust yourself and others
Continue to dream of collective liberation

—scott crow[2]

Perhaps it is more important to be in community, vulnerable and real and whole, than to be right, or to be winning.

—adrienne maree brown[3]

Trust and responsibility as common notions

I t is clear that capitalism—administered by left- and right-wing governments—is a disaster for people, non-humans, and the earth. However, cynicism and disillusionment do not necessarily lead to revolt or struggle. Empire's capacity for decentralized control no longer relies on legitimacy or faith. We do not have to believe capitalism is good for us or that the state will help and protect us, so long as we remain enmeshed in Empire's radical monopoly over life, from schooling to law to the built environment that surrounds us.

In this chapter, we suggest that *trust and responsibility* are emerging in Empire's cracks. This is not about one way of trusting or a fixed set of responsibilities but about the proliferation of different forms. A lot of what we get at in this chapter comes from carla's longstanding involvement in youth and kids' liberation movements, which fundamentally upend some of the basic assumptions embedded in many forms of organizing. To create intergenerational spaces where kids can thrive means holding space for play and emergence by warding off the twin pitfalls of individualism and conformity. This requires nurturing a baseline of trust, responsibility, and autonomy. We also draw on other movements that we have learned from and been challenged by, including Indigenous resurgence, transformative justice, and anti-violence, all of which emphasize the importance of relationship-based trust and responsibility.

Many of the most militant movements and insurrectionary spaces have emphasized trust as an indispensable

part of their capacity to resist Empire and defend their insurgent forms of life. For instance, speaking of autonomous
spaces carved out by anarchists in Greece, Tasos Sagris has
suggested that "the main organizational form in Greece is
friendship. We believe that friendship will be revolutionary. Very close, very good loving friends, that like each other,
that spend their lives together, they trust one another. This
is a part of the insurrection."[4] Similarly, Marina Sitrin argues
that "groups that are grounded in trust and affect tend to
be more militant. This is especially true for the recuperated
workplaces in Argentina, and they reflect directly upon this.
Knowing one another and working together for years built
up a trust that helped when the time came to defend their
workplaces physically (with molotovs, slingshots, etc.)."[5]
Across North America and beyond, many Indigenous peoples are clear that their militancy stems from a responsibility
to protect Indigenous land and life, animated by grounded
normativities that we explored in the last chapter.

So what does it mean to nurture trust and responsibility? What do these concepts even mean today? Often
"trust" is a catch-all word that suggests there is only one
all-or-nothing way to trust, and this is part of the problem. Similarly, responsibility can be turned into a reductive
set of stifling norms or duties. We want to walk with these
questions: Are there different kinds of trust? What makes
it possible to trust people up front, without knowing them
well? What does a joyful responsibility look and feel like?
How can trust and responsibility be conceived and lived in
ways that are open and enabling rather than being imposed
as fixed moral duties?

We suggest that these transformative capacities are not based in rigid ideologies or fixed ways of being. Joyful transformation is nurtured through what Spinoza called *common notions*: shared values and sensibilities that are flexible and based in relationships with human and non-human others. The concept of common notions has been elaborated by Gilles Deleuze and by a current of contemporary radical intellectuals in Spain and Argentina, including Sebastián Touza, whom we interviewed for this book.[6] Touza's work explains that we might experience joy—a growth in our powers—as a sudden flash but be unsure what made it possible or how to support more joyful encounters and relations. This is the *passive* experience of joy. The passage from passivity to activity happens through the formation of common notions: people figuring out together what sustains transformation in their situations and how to move with it and participate in its unfolding. Common notions can never be a fixed way of doing things or a guarantee that things will go well. They can sound idealistic, but in fact they are the opposite: they are pragmatic sensibilities, *material* conceptions that arise out of embodied, mutually enabling face-to-face relationships. Touza writes,

> This is because, in Spinoza's ethics, to have notions in common, people require more than the sole agreement between the rational ideas that come out of their minds. Common notions are formed in the local and concrete terrain of affects that emerge in the encounter between bodies. A common notion

is a bond formed by reciprocal affect. Joy enables a
leap beyond the world of sad passions.[7]

Common notions are slippery because, like joy itself,
they emerge from concrete, unique situations. To share
them with others whose situations are composed differently, then, is precarious and fraught. Detached from the
circumstances and practices that birthed them, common
notions can turn into moral commandments or stagnant habits rather than ways of relating that remain alive
through struggle and care.

As common notions, trust and responsibility are
emergent values connected to specific practices, movements, and forms of life. A learned trust—in situations, in
others, and in one's own capacities—is in this sense an unfolding process. To trust in transformation is to undo fear
and control. Similarly, the forms of responsibility we are
discussing are not enshrined in law and formal agreements
but emerge instead through a sense of feeling invited to
participate in the world, care for others and be cared for,
and support and be supported.

(Mis)trust and (ir)responsibility under Empire

Working through trust and responsibility is difficult
because both of these words have been so thoroughly
colonized by Empire. An important place to begin, we
think, is with the ways that Empire sows mistrust and
destroys our capacity for collective responsibility by

making us dependent on its destructive, depleting, violent ways of life.

Many people's impulse is to mistrust others from the start, and it makes sense, given that many of us have been living Hobbes's dream, made real, for centuries. Most everyone we know has been touched by some kind of oppression and abuse, and Empire's oppressive divisions often lead people to betray even their most intimate relations. For instance, feminists have coined the term "gaslighting" to get at a common patriarchal dynamic that undermines the perceptions of women and femmes by second-guessing, explaining away, and denying their experiences and insights. Gaslighting can be subtle and unintentional, but as feminist writer Nora Samaran explains, it is particularly insidious because it undermines people's trust in their own capacities:

> If you think of the power, the strength, the capacity to effect change that women who trust themselves are capable of, what we are losing when we doubt ourselves is an indomitable force for social change that is significant and therefore, to some, frightening. In other words, our capacity to know ourselves is immensely powerful.[8]

All forms of oppression seem to have this tendency: racism, heteropatriarchy, ableism, ageism, colonization, and other systems of oppression contort people's insights, experiences, and differences into weaknesses or deny them outright. For this reason, the emergence of trust can be a powerful weapon, which is being recovered all the time through struggle.

For many of us, mistrust in ourselves and others started when we were kids, and in a lot of cases in our homes. When they're really young, kids are curious, open, vulnerable, and capable of radically trusting those around them, and this tends to get sucked out of them from many directions by Empire and the kinds of hierarchical and competitive relationships it promotes. One of the most damaging forms of distrust is built into modern disciplinary institutions, schooling in particular. As organizer and scholar Matt Hern writes,

> At school children are always monitored, and schooled parents believe that they should similarly be constantly monitoring their offspring, in the name of safety. The last decades of this century has seen an exponential growth in concern for children's daily safety, particularly in cities, and most parents I come into contact with want to keep a very close eye on their kids. This is a laudable concern, and one I share, yet I have a deep suspicion of the equation that safety = surveillance. There is a threshold where our concerned eye becomes over-monitoring and disabling, an authoritarian presence shaping our kids' lives.[9]

Hern is not singling out certain parents as oppressive, and he implicates himself in this too. He is pointing to the collective inheritance of a way of life that divorces people from their capacities to trust each other. The model for inculcating these values was (and is) intense discipline and control: kids are encased in concrete for over a decade, trained to sit still, memorize, and obey authority. As the political theorist Toby Rollo has argued, it is no coincidence that colonization, racism, heteropatriarchy, and ableism all tell stories that constitute oppressed and dispossessed people as *children*.[10] Empire conceives its Others as untrustworthy and lacking maturity, health, morality, knowledge, civilization, and rationality, and so they have all been targets for education, confinement, and control—or for total eradication and genocide.

Empire's radical monopoly over life

Ivan Illich was a prominent radical intellectual in the 1970s, but aside from his radical critique of schooling, he is not well-known today. For Illich, modern schooling was only one of the many ways that dependence was being entrenched—a dependence not only on capitalist production and consumption but also on a whole violent, industrialized, disciplined, and controlled way of life. His concept of *radical monopoly* points to something more systematic than the control over a particular market by a particular firm. Instead, radical monopoly gets at the way that Empire monopolizes *life itself*: how people relate to each other, how they get around, how they get their sustenance, and the whole texture of everyday life. A world built for cars forces out other ways of moving, and modern building codes and bylaws make it impossible and illegal for people to build their own dwellings or even to live together at all if they cannot pass as a nuclear family. Modern medicine does not just create a new way of understanding the body: its scientific understanding is premised on a radical monopoly over health and the subjugation (or commodification) of other healing traditions. To be healthy under Empire is to be a properly functioning, able-bodied, neurotypical individual capable of work, and to be sick often means becoming medicalized: isolated, confined, and dependent on strangers and experts. Law, policing, and prisons monopolize the field of justice by enforcing cycles of punishment and incarceration, forcing out the capacity of people to protect each other and resolve conflicts themselves. The rise of industrial agriculture has been accompanied by a loss of the convivial relations surrounding subsistence: the connection to the growing and processing of food, the intimacy with ecosystems and seasons it entails, and the collective rituals, celebrations, and practices that have accompanied these traditions. Empire's infrastructure induces dependence on forms of production, specialized knowledge, expertise, and tools that detach people from their capacities to learn, grow, build, produce, and take care of each other.

Since Illich wrote, these monopolies have folded into ever more diffuse and generalized forms of control, sunk deeper into the fabric of life. Deleuze called this new form of power taking shape over the course of the nineteenth and twentieth centuries "control societies."[11] Rather than telling people exactly what to do, this mode of power *regularizes* life, calling forth certain ways of living and feeling, and making other forms of life die. Surveillance no longer ends when one exits a particular institution: through social media, smartphones, browsing histories, and credit cards, surveillance is ubiquitous, continuous, and increasingly *participatory*. We are enjoined to share, consume, and express ourselves, and every choice feeds back into algorithms that predict our habits and preferences with ever increasing precision. The performance of self-expression is constantly encouraged, and as the Institute for Precarious Consciousness writes, "Our success in this performance in turn affects everything from our ability to access human warmth to our ability to access means of subsistence, not just in the form of the wage but also in the form of credit."[12] Under this apparatus, there is little room for silence, nuance, listening, exploration, or the rich subtleties of tone and body language. Anything too intense or subversive is either incorporated or surgically removed by security, police, or emergency personnel. Class, anti-Blackness, Islamophobia, ableism, and other structured forms of violence are coded into the algorithms that make everyone a potential terrorist, thief, or error. Even those who are supposed to enjoy the most—those who can afford the newest screens and the most expensive forms of consumption—are inducted into a state of nearly constant distraction, numbness, and anxiety.

Perpetual individualization obscures the crushing *collective* effects of Empire. When this form of control is working, interactions are hypervisible, superficial, predictable, and self-managed. To be constantly mistrusted and controlled is also to be detached from one's own capacity to experiment, make mistakes, and learn without instruction or coercion. To internalize the responsibilities of neoliberal individualism is to sink into the mesh of control and subjection. The responsible economic subject owns her own property, pays her own debts, invests in her future, and meets her needs and desires through consumption. She is individually responsible for her health, her economic situation, her life prospects, and even her emotional states. These forms of subjection make it difficult to imagine—let alone participate in—collective alternatives. From the dependence on armed strangers to resolve conflicts, to the hum of an extraction-fuelled world, to the glow of screens that beckon attention, to the stranglehold of policy and bureaucracy, to the intergenerational violence and abuse that permeate lovers and families, Empire is constantly entrenching dependence on a world that makes joy, trust, and responsibility difficult.

It is not a question of revealing this to people, as if they are dupes. Struggling amid these forms of control means grappling with their affective hold on us and our daily lives. Anxiety, addiction, and depression are not merely secrets to reveal or illusions to dispel. Preaching about Empire's horrors can stoke cynicism or ironic detachment rather than undoing subjection. One can still feel bound and depleted, despite one's awareness. Empire's subjects are "free" to be mistrustful and resentful of the system under which they live. One can hate Empire as much as one wants, as long as one continues to work, pay rent, and consume. There is no simple correspondence between intentions and actions, as if the problem is simply figuring out what to do and doing it. Undoing subjection is not about conscious opposition or finding a way to be happy amid misery. Challenging Empire's radical monopoly over life means interrupting its affective and infrastructural hold, undoing some of our existing attachments and desires, and creating new ones.

Towards conviviality

> Most people who have lived through any moment
> where formal institutions of power go away, or are
> forced away, agree with this point. When left alone,
> when left with one another, people turn to one another
> and use forms of mutual aid and support. The wake of
> the break is a beautiful opening up of possibility.
>   —Marina Sitrin[13]

At Empire's edges, in its cracks, people are finding each other, recovering subjugated knowledges, revaluing their own traditions, pushing back against discipline and control. In dramatic uprisings and slow shifts, people are reconnecting with their own powers and capacities to make, act, live, and fight together. *Conviviality* is the name that Illich gives to ways of life that promote flourishing, which are being squeezed out by Empire:

> I choose the term "conviviality" to designate the
> opposite of industrial productivity. I intend it to
> mean autonomous and creative intercourse among

> persons, and the intercourse of persons with their environment; and this in contrast with the conditioned response of persons to the demands made upon them by others and by a man-made environment. I consider conviviality to be individual freedom realized in personal interdependence and, as such, an intrinsic ethical value.[14]

Illich's conception of conviviality resonates with the relational form of freedom we explored in the last chapter. Conviviality names the creative relationships that emerge between people and their material surroundings, sustained by grassroots trust and responsibility.[15] In other words, it is Illich's name for joy sustained by common notions. Conviviality helps clarify that joy is not simply something felt by an individual but also the effect of enabling assemblages of bodies, tools, gestures, and relationships. It is not about a utopian future or a romantic past but about breaking from dependence on Empire's stifling infrastructures. This is most evident after natural disasters and during insurrections, when some of Empire's radical monopolies are dramatically short-circuited.

While these situations often trigger elite fear-mongering and fascist vigilantism, they are also spaces where joyful and convivial forms of life blossom, as people discover—in haphazard, decentralized, and emergent ways—how to live without Empire's crushing monopolies. Here is what one anonymous participant had to say about their experience of the uprising in Cairo, Egypt, where people famously took over Tahrir Square:

Cairo was never more alive than during the first
Tahrir Square. Since nothing was functioning any-
more, everyone took care of what was around them.
People took charge of the garbage collecting, swept
the walkways and sometimes even repainted them;
they drew frescos on the walls and they looked after
each other. Even the traffic had become miraculous-
ly fluid, since there were no more traffic control-
lers. What we suddenly realized is that we had been
robbed of our simplest gestures, those that make
the city ours and make it something we belong to.
At Tahrir Square, people would arrive and sponta-
neously ask themselves what they could do to help.
They would go to the kitchen, or to stretcher the
wounded, work on banners or shields or slingshots,
join discussions, make up songs. We realized that
the state organization was actually the maximum
disorganization, because it depended on negating
the human ability to self-organize. At Tahrir, no
one gave any orders. Obviously, if someone had got
it in their heads to organize all that, it would have
immediately turned into chaos.[16]

Similar accounts can be found by people who have
lived through disasters and insurrections throughout the
world. For example, the upwelling of autonomy, experimentation, and joy was palpable in the Argentinean uprising
that began in 2001. While corporate media and politicians
framed it as a chaotic, short-lived riot, Marina Sitrin has
shown how autonomous forms of life have endured, despite

challenges, for over a decade.[17] Workers have taken over factories and learned to run them collectively, without bosses, through a process of *autogestion*, or worker self-management. This is not merely a transition from top-down factory production to cooperative production but also a process of transformative struggle in which whole neighborhoods defended factories against police and capitalists. Similarly, the neighborhood assemblies that formed through the uprising have created new ways for people to resolve conflicts and support each other without relying on the state.

Anywhere that Empire's form of life is suspended, emergent capacities to live otherwise rush in. Through struggle and experimentation, people formulate problems and respond to them together, taking responsibility for collective work and care, and bonds of trust take hold.

Rebecca Solnit speaks to the emergence of conviviality and joy amid disasters in her book *A Paradise Built in Hell*:

> In the wake of an earthquake, a bombing, or a major storm, most people are altruistic, urgently engaged in caring for themselves and those around them, strangers and neighbors as well as friends and loved ones. The image of the selfish, panicky, or regressive savage human being has little truth to it.[18]

Solnit documents and interviews the survivors of several disasters, including earthquakes and hurricanes, economic collapses, and terrorist attacks. Consistently she finds that in the wake of disaster it is mainly elites who panic and resort to violence. Furthermore, bureaucratic disaster relief tends to entrench misery and despair. At the same time, in the midst of intense suffering and pain, large numbers of people engage in mutual aid and solidarity. In fact, many people reflect on their experiences of earthquakes, hurricanes, and even bombings as joyful experiences in the Spinozan sense, in which they feel more alive and connected to others. Without top-down organization or bureaucracies, they coordinate food and medical supplies, take care of injured and sick people, and defend themselves in ways that are decentralized but not disorganized.

Why is there joy in disaster? Solnit suggests that it is because Empire's debilitating monopolies on life are suspended: "If paradise now arises in hell, it's because in the suspension of the usual order and the failure of most systems, we are free to live and act in another way."[19] Solnit is not arguing that we should wish for disasters. What her argument exposes is that everyday life under Empire is *already* a certain kind of ongoing and seemingly intractable disaster, in a world where distraction, anxiety, individualism, and dependence have become normalized. What is enlivening about disasters is the emergent capacity they unleash for trust, responsibility, care, and simply *being present and feeling connected*.

The upwelling of conviviality and joyful forms of life is only one tendency among others in situations where control is abated. Alongside these are other tendencies: waves of sexualized violence, hoarding, bunkerism, fascist vigilantes, intimidation and violence from military and police, and desires for control based in fear and mistrust. To reinstall its rhythms, Empire must turn these moments into situations of extreme deprivation and violence so that its subjects can only experience the suspension of control as a horrifying prospect. The bubbling up of decentralized, convivial forms of life must be crushed as quickly as possible, and "order" must be restored. In this sense, Empire's means of counter-insurgency include not only police repression but also the liquidation of emergent orders, the stoking of divisions and terror, and the reinstallation of individualizing and isolating forms of life. People go back to their jobs, their houses, their smartphones, and control returns.

But never completely. A key question is how to keep these relations alive in everyday life, even as Empire's stultifying rhythms are reimposed. Among the stakes in these struggles, as we have suggested, is their potential to elicit responsiveness as people are drawn out of themselves and their routines. In an interview with Naomi Klein, Leanne Simpson insists that responsibility and reciprocity are the alternatives to settler colonial extractivism:

NAOMI: If extractivism is a mindset, a way of looking at the world, what is the alternative?
LEANNE: Responsibility. Because I think when people extract things, they're taking and they're running and they're using it for just their own good. What's missing is the re-sponsibility. If you're not developing relationships with the people, you're not giving back, you're not sticking around to see the impact of the extraction. You're moving to some-place else. The alternative is deep reciprocity. It's respect, it's relationship, it's responsibility, and it's local. If you're forced to stay in your 50-mile radius, then you very much

are going to experience the impacts of extractivist behavior. The only way you can shield yourself from that is when you get your food from around the world or from someplace else. So the more distance and the more globalization then the more shielded I am from the negative impacts of extractivist behavior.[20]

To be more responsible and self-reliant in this way is not to inhabit the neoliberal ideal of the individual, nor is it an isolationist independence. Protecting ecosystems and nonhuman life from devastation is often cast in terms of conservation, austerity, or a new mode of management. But these tendencies exist in tension with the grassroots recovery and reinvention of ways of living that support human *and* nonhuman life, through ongoing and intimate contact with natural processes. This is not about protecting a separate "environment" but nurturing forms of life that persist through interdependent relationships: soil, water, plants, and animals are not resources to be exploited or managed but an interconnected web that people can participate in and enrich. As people regain intimate contact with the places where they live, they get to know the way the water flows when it rains, the plants that grow up together and how they are used by birds and wasps and bees, the way that the sun warms a south-facing slope where different plants thrive.

This brings abstract concepts like climate change and biodiversity loss down to a practical scale, felt through interactions with the sensible world rather than intellectualized through statistics. Supporting these relationships might entail intense grief and rage: one discovers that a childhood hideout among trees has been paved over; the absence of once-familiar birds and bees is felt; one finds cancerous fish and dried-up creeks. There are overwhelming and heartbreaking changes taking place, and being connected to communities of plants and animals makes it as painful as it is nourishing. It is from this place that joyful responses to ecological catastrophes are emerging. Not happy or optimistic responses, but capacities to respond to the horrors in ways based in lived and ever-changing relationships.

Emergent trust and responsibility: three examples

Indigenous struggles

In North America, the recovery of responsibility and interconnectedness is expressed most deeply and forcefully in Indigenous resurgence and other struggles where people are reasserting a profound land-based knowledge, revaluing traditions that have accrued through generations of reciprocal relationships with land. It is no coincidence that Indigenous peoples have been behind the most durable and militant resistance to ecological devastation, including pipelines, dams, logging, tar sands, fracking, and other forms of resource extraction. To be immersed in a web of reciprocal relationships is also to feel the responsibility to protect that web.

The Unist'ot'en Camp, for instance, is an Indigenous-led project that for years has been successfully resisting proposed fracked gas pipelines that would cross the territories of the Wet'suwet'en people in British Columbia. The grassroots Wet'suwet'en people leading the project have been clear that they are not protesting pipelines but reasserting their traditional responsibilities to take care of their territories, and re-establishing traditional protocols for entry. Several years ago, they created a checkpoint and began turning away those working for surveyors and others involved in pipeline construction, while inviting thousands of supporters onto their territories. Mel Bazil, a long-term supporter and a Gitxsan relative of the Unist'ot'en clan, speaks to the power of these land-based responsibilities:

> It's a reciprocal culture; it never really ended.... To share that knowledge outwardly to other grassroots folks—migrants and grassroots settlers, as well as other Indigenous nations—it's been very, very powerful to see our people come together. Not just in the face of devastation and destruction, but to survive and to understand each other.[21]

Not only have they been successful in halting pipeline construction; in the process, the Unist'ot'en Camp has constructed permaculture gardens, and a healing center and hosted annual action camps where hundreds of Indigenous and non-Indigenous supporters come from across North America (and elsewhere) to connect with each other, explore affinities, and deepen networks of trust and mutual support.

Similar processes are taking place at other camps across territories claimed by British Columbia and beyond, including the Madii Lii Camp and Lax Kw'alaams's defense of Lelu Island, both part of a network of front lines committed to stopping pipelines and fracked gas expansion. Furthermore, as we write this, there is a local and worldwide proliferation of solidarity actions, fund-raisers, and on-the-ground support for the Standing Rock Sioux Tribe's resistance to the Dakota Access Pipeline.

Among non-Indigenous people, we also see expressions of land-connected responsibilities in the spread of communal gardening, environmental and climate justice, permaculture, regenerative farming, grassroots bioremediation, resistance to resource extraction, and animal liberation struggles, among others. Many of these struggles are simultaneously fighting the ecological devastation of Empire and its brutal forms of control and exploitation while making space for convivial forms of life.

Anti-violence and transformative justice

This renewal of collective responsibility and trust can also be seen in feminist, anti-violence, and transformative justice movements that address interpersonal violence in ways that undo the monopoly of policing and courts. A crucial insight from these movements is that listening to, believing, and trusting survivors of violence is powerful, undermining a culture that normalizes violence and blames survivors of rape and abuse for the ways they have been hurt. The capacity of survivors to trust themselves and each other is often the beginning of community-based responses through which people take collective responsibility for confronting and transforming patterns of violence.

The work of these movements has led to a proliferation of networks of mutual support and care and the creation of alternatives to police, courts, and prisons that exacerbate violence and oppression. In North America, these initiatives have been led by BIPOC women, Two-Spirit, queer, and trans people, in particular, whose communities have been targeted with criminalization and incarceration since the inception of policing and prisons. As INCITE! and Critical Resistance organizers write,

> The reliance on the criminal justice system has taken power away from women's ability to organize collectively to stop violence and has invested this power within the state. The result is that women who seek redress in the criminal justice system feel disempowered and alienated. It has also promoted an individualistic approach toward ending violence such that the only way people think they can intervene in stopping violence is to call the police. This reliance has shifted our focus from developing ways communities can collectively respond to violence.[22]

In this context, "transformative justice" (TJ) has emerged as an alternative to "restorative justice" models. Its emphasis on transformation is based on the insight that—especially among Black and Indigenous communities—violence is structural and institutional, without a baseline that could be "restored." Instead, as lawyer and anti-violence organizer Rachel Zellars explains, it works pragmatically from existing relationships to interrupt institutional and interpersonal cycles of violence, disposability, and punishment:

> [Transformative justice] centres Black women's experiences of violence while resisting the notion that speaking about violence detracts from organizing: men who cause harm can be understood simultaneously as effective or well-loved organizers and as perpetrators of misogynistic violence. In this sense, TJ is open-armed – naming violence committed while leaving room for those who have caused harm to be accountable and to come back into the fold."[23]

Transformative justice and anti-violence are also linked to struggles for migrant justice, anti-gentrification, and prison abolition. In Halifax, Nova Scotia, women refugees created an informal support group and drop-in center for those in their community facing domestic abuse, which led to a cooperative catering business and a childcare network that helped address the poverty and isolation that was re-creating the conditions for violence.[24] In 2004 anti-violence advocate Mimi Kim founded Creative Interventions, an organization dedicated to sharing grassroots responses to interpersonal violence and lessons from these attempts.[25] Forged in alliance and conversation with prison abolitionist movements, they encourage reliance on friends, family, neighbors, and coworkers as alternatives to professional services or policing. Their flexible approach acknowledges that people may want to remain in their relationships or the places where they live, centering the needs of survivors while working towards the transformation of the situation that led to the violence.

By enacting alternatives to cops and courts, these initiatives nurture autonomy in place of racist, heteropatriarchal institutions, undoing the culture in which both survivors and perpetrators are made disposable and institutional violence is obscured. Everyone we know who is involved in these efforts to end cycles of violence can attest to how fraught, messy, and difficult they can be. They do not always go well. Nonetheless, this is the kind of "freedom" discussed in the last chapter: the capacity to work on relationships, to become more active in undoing oppressive patterns, and to nurture and deepen trust and collective responsibility.

Deschooling and youth liberation

A third convivial current is deschooling and youth liberation and the proliferation of alternatives to schooling that are led by kids and youth, including those who are in school. The Purple Thistle, co-created with youth in Vancouver, Canada, has been a vibrant example of this: it nurtured a space for youth not only to hang out but also to experiment and learn together without being controlled and supervised, to take collective responsibility for running the space, and to build strong bonds with each other.

The youth-run projects included a community garden, screenprinting, photography, graffiti, zine publishing, discussion groups, filmmaking, animation, film nights, a radical library, sound and music recording, graphic design, fiber and textile arts, and more. These initiatives were emergent, based on people's desires and priorities. carla was the "director" of the Thistle from 2009 until it closed in spring 2015, but her job was basically to do the bulk of the paperwork, support and mentor when asked, and to work as a kind of matchmaker connecting youth to mentors and apprenticeships, both formal and informal. Overall, carla's role as director was to function as an anchor to support the fluid and flexible relationships at the heart of the Thistle. Other adults also supported the Thistle as anchors, co-directors, and mentors, but all day-to-day decisions were made by the youth-run collective and the various pods that sprang from it. As Matt Hern, Thistle co-founder and director before carla, said of the project,

> I like to think of the Thistle as being really easy in the way that school is hard and really hard in the way that school is easy. So, you go to school for example, or you go to a workplace, or you go to many institutions, you know exactly what you have to do, you know what's expected of you, you don't really have to think a whole lot. And that's nice sometimes; you just walk through it: essentially just follow orders and do what you're told and you'll be fine. So it's really easy in lots of ways. It's also very difficult because that's really hard for most people, and because you fight against it and you resist, but the Thistle turns that on its ass in

lots of ways. So it's really easy because no one is
telling you what to do, you can do whatever you
like, you can come and go as you like, you can figure out how you can access it. So it's very easy but
it's also very difficult, 'cause that's a tremendous
kind of responsibility.[26]

The Thistle can be understood as a counter-institu-
tion, a flexible container where the participants themselves
shaped roles and responsibilities in an open, experimental
way. Such counter-institutions can prefigure trust and conviviality, creating space where these ways of relating can be
tried out, become patterns and habits, and eventually take
hold in new communities and projects.

Many of these relationships ran outside the walls of the
Thistle but were nevertheless vital for creating webs of care
and mutual aid. For example, when individuals or groups
found themselves in dicey or difficult situations, folks could
lean on each other rather than call the cops. Often this
meant supporting someone to get the care they actually
needed instead of being thrown into the criminal system.
Other times it meant creating space for accountability to
take hold. These forms of trust and responsibility never
crystallized into a public website, handbook, or formal organization; they were relational and ad hoc. We think that
people are doing this all the time. In fact, in order to keep
it safer for many to engage in these ways, and to hold on
to these values as common notions, institutionalization or
publicity is often avoided.

The power of baseline trust

> I think we cannot have any kind of trust in a mass of
> 100 million individuals, they will produce the horror.
> But if we bring everything to the human scale, to the
> communities, to small groups of people, then we can
> really trust that the people will have the wisdom to dis-
> cuss and to generate consensus.
>
> —Gustavo Esteva[27]

We have argued that Empire's institutions are a ceaseless attack on conviviality, and we want to hold on to emergent
forms of trust and responsibility as common notions. In
this context, we want to share an excerpt from our interview with Kelsey Cham C.:

CARLA AND NICK: Can you talk about the potential of trusting folks
up front and how you saw it play out at the Thistle?
KELSEY: Yeah, totally, I think that's awesome. Actually I think
you [carla] were one of the first people to actually trust me
without even knowing me. And I was like, what the hell?
Why? Why? How do you know I'm not gonna just fuck
everything up and run away and steal a bunch of money
and go? How do you know that? But in trusting me, I
was like, holy shit: I trust this situation and this collective
twenty times more and I want to give back to it because
I've been given this opportunity to do something that I've
never been able to do before, which is awesome. But I have
been thinking about trust and how with trauma we build

all these walls and we start to mistrust everything—I have
a pretty hard time trusting people—there's a point where
I'm like, this is too personal and too intimate, and now my
walls are going to go up. I was sitting and thinking about
how... probably one of the best ways to break down the
walls of the system is to break down the walls around each
other first, and I think the only way we can break down
those walls is with trust. And that's the core thing you said.

Joyful militancy and trust, and compassion, and humility are all tied together: in other cultures, traditional
cultures—I don't know a lot about this—but from what I
know, older Indigenous cultures have these ideas of respect,
humility, compassion, and I think in karate I've seen it,
and it's funny because karate is a martial art, a fighting tool,
and one of the things that we learn is that we have to love
everyone, including our opponents. And that's the toughest
thing to say in this community. People are like, "what the
fuck, how can you say that, you can't just love your abuser."
And it's true, I can't just let go of everything. It's not that,
it's being compassionate, I think, to situations.

CARLA AND NICK: Can we have the expectation of trust up front?
Is it an alternative to the idea that trust always needs to be
earned?

KELSEY: Yeah, that's like our society: you gotta earn everything;
you earn money, you build trust and respect. You gotta
prove to me that I should trust you or respect you. And
that's an interesting point; I have a tough time with that,
trusting people. But I think it's a feedback system: probably
the more you allow yourself to trust people initially, probably the more well-reciprocated that will be. I felt it: you

trust me and I didn't understand it. That's how fucked up our system is. Even though I didn't do anything wrong or to harm you, I didn't understand how someone could trust me without knowing me first.[28]

At the core of this conversation is the potential—never an obligation or guarantee—of trusting people up front. In a practical sense, it's our experience that when people offer trust up front, most people rise to the occasion. Without turning it into a commandment that everyone should follow, we want to affirm the ways that expanding up-front trust can be transformative and enabling. It can feel strange and scary to be in situations where people think well of us and trust us to do our best, without having to "earn it" or "prove it," but it also can be incredibly freeing, making us feel more capable. This is a trust not only in individuals, but in unfolding processes with open-ended potential, without fixed rules. In this sense, it is trust in joy: in emergent capacities to increase collective powers of acting.

But what does this look like? It happens in all kinds of subtle, relational ways. One of the things that made the Thistle different from many other youth projects was that everyone in the collective had keys to the space and were free to use them anytime. No one had to go through a formal interview process or sign over their life to have a set. Many bureaucratic procedures like this are based in distrust, as are many radical spaces that replicate institutional norms of Empire. But this up-front trust also entailed responsibility: it required that folks met regularly to check in, talk about how things were going, and so on.

These practices helped to create an environment of shared connection and kindness, a space filled with friendship and mutual support, and ultimately a place to build community.

When we have been involved in movements, spaces, and forms of life imbued with this sense of trust, along with a fierce sense of mutual responsibility, we have noticed that it gave us an ability to be brave, to try new things, to be vulnerable, and to take risks. This is not a politics of "let's all get along" pacifism. Writing in the context of collective resistance to evictions in the United States, Sitrin argues that trust is intimately connected to direct action:

> It is not only about changing relationships and "feeling good" but inextricably linked to direct action. It is about creating the alternatives that we now desire and need. It is using the base of trust so as to occupy homes and prevent foreclosures and evictions, all the while knowing that to call on one's neighbor means they will come out and support you—as has been done many hundreds of times throughout the US in only the past few months. People doing eviction defense in support of their neighbors even speak of how they might not have "liked" that particular person, but that they "felt" a connection to them and cared so much about what happened to them that they were risking possible arrest by putting their bodies between the marshals and the person's home. From these relationships, in dozens and dozens of neighborhoods and communities across the country, networks of support and care have been formed.

Neighbors go door-to-door to let others know that they can (and will) be defended if they need it, and also to just share stories, food, and support.[29]

These conceptions of care, trust, and openness are not new ideas. On the contrary, Gustavo Esteva and Madhu Prakash argue that what they call *hospitality*—a radical openness, generosity, and trust in others—is common among many traditions that have not been lost to bureaucratic institutions, industrial dependence, and other trappings of "development." Among those less entangled in Empire's radical monopolies, hospitality remains alive:

> Common people learn to trust each other and be trustworthy in ways that are rapidly vanishing among the "social minorities." Their common faith is seldom deposited in abstract causes or phantoms, like human kind. Instead, it is entrusted to real men and women, defining the place to which they belong and that belongs to them. Rather than the private hope and public despair of the "social minorities" (some hope for their personal lives, no hope for public affairs) ... we usually find expressed among them a common hope in their own capacity to deal with their predicaments, whether good, bad or indifferent. Given that condition, they can be both hospitable and responsible.[30]

The notion of hospitality is not just about welcoming guests; it connotes a sensibility of trust based on people's sense of their capacity to face the world together. Being held in this way also enables people to be open to strangers: not simply "tolerant" but capable of open-ended encounters, generosity, and curiosity. To encounter a stranger and be open to difference in this way is not at all the same as tolerance. Liberal tolerance treats individuals as atomized entities who are required to put up with each other, with the state as a universal arbiter. Hospitality starts not from rights-bearing individuals but from a sensuous and lively world, composed through common notions that have evolved to sustain joy or conviviality. To be "hosted" is to be allowed to encounter a world, to be invited into it. For the same reason, it is not individuals who are trusting; there is no self-enclosed individual who "chooses" to trust but bundles of relationships in which the capacity for trust is activated and drawn out of people.

This is not a romanticization of "premodern" or "pre-industrial" cultures but a recognition that Empire's radical monopolies are uneven and contested. Esteva and Prakash insist that people are always recovering, sustaining, and reinventing convivial forms of life. This can be seen in insurrectionary spaces, in disasters, in a whole multiplicity of projects and struggles: anywhere that people find the capacity to formulate problems together and carve out some wiggle room from Empire's monopoly over life.

Infinite trust and responsibilities?

Trust and responsibility are composed differently based in the contexts from which they emerge. They can be conceived as a set of questions, including the capacity to *selectively* extend trust across the divisions of race, class, sex, gender, colonization, ability, age, and other forms of oppression and division.

There are good reasons why trust may be difficult. Distrust is often based on experiences of abuse, violation, or being used or taken advantage of. A lot of women, genderqueer, and trans folks don't trust cis-gendered men, people of color are often wary of white people, and Indigenous people refuse to trust settlers. These are not ideological prejudices but strategies of survival.

Moreover, to talk about trust and responsibility can sound naïve or just plain stupid in a world in which individual responsibility is callously imposed and so much violence happens to trusting people. At the same time, we want to recognize that people are constantly building trust across these divisions, in ways that open potentials for new relationships. In this sense, a crucial component of joyful militancy is a collective capacity to *build, maintain, and repair* trust, which may entail taking responsibility for harm, disrespect, or complicity with Empire in ways that we may not have anticipated. Richard Day suggests that many antiauthoritarian currents today are animated by what he calls "infinite responsibility":

> This means that as individuals, as groups, we can never allow ourselves to think that we are 'done', that we have identified all of the sites, structures, and processes of oppression 'out there' or 'in here', inside our own individual and group identities.

> Infinite responsibility means always being ready
> to hear another other, a subject who by definition
> does not 'exist', indeed must not exist (be heard) if
> current relations of power are to be maintained.[31]

In this sense, the questions of what we are responsible for, whom we are responsible to, and what we can be held accountable for are always open, ethical questions. This does not mean that they will be completely revised at any second but that they are never completely fixed, held open by an ethical responsiveness. Responsibility is infinite in the sense that it is unbounded: we can harm each other in unforeseen ways, and infinite responsibility gestures at the potential of remaining responsive to this. As a way of furthering this line of thought, responsibility could be broken apart into *response-ability*. Writer and facilitator Zainab Amadahy writes,

> Responsibility in this sense is not a burden but
> something that actually enhances our life experi-
> ence. The word literally means "ability to respond."
> In the relational framework we might understand
> responsibility as the ability to respond appropri-
> ately – that is, for the common good. In this sense,
> responsibility is seen as preferable to individualism,
> which doesn't really exist.[32]

This "common good" is not an abstract good based in Western morality. For Amadahy, it is based in attunement to human and nonhuman relationships and the capacity to support them. Following this line, responsibility is ethical rather than moral. As soon as answers to these questions become permanent, the ethical moment is gone, and one cannot be responsive to relationships in motion.

Like all common notions, trust and responsibility are not guarantees that things will go well or that oppression and violence will not happen. Trust, hospitality, and openness are precious and important precisely *because* they entail incredible courage and risk, especially in the context of Empire, with its many layers of violence and control. For this reason, Esteva and Prakash write that "nothing is more treacherous than that which violates hospitality."[33] To be open and vulnerable entails the risk of being hurt and betrayed in ways that we cannot be if we are on guard or closed-off. Pointing to the need for openness is not an injunction to remain open to everything. Instead, it is another open-ended ethical question about where, when, with whom, and how to be open and trusting.

Holding common notions gently

Trust and responsibility are slippery for a number of reasons. They are not simply the result of rational thinking or even a combination of theory and practice, because they are implicated in affect: they come out of thinking *and feeling* the transformative encounters with our own power and the powers of others.

This is part of why it is so important to hold on to trust and responsibility as common notions rather than prescriptions. Common notions emerge from the upwellings of joy that make them possible, as people (re)learn together how to nurture convivial forms of life. To turn trust into an imperative is to rob it of this potential. Still, even among the people who generated them, common notions can be converted into rigid doctrines that drain away joyful transformation rather than supporting it. This happens when certainty arises about the only way forward, when "trust me" and "take responsibility" become injunctions. This turns them into dead words, lifted from the tangle of transformative movement that brought them into being. Common notions can only be held gently, as flexible ideas whose power lives within the relationships and processes they sustain.

The slippage from common notions to set principles is all too common among radical movements and milieus, especially in North America. We think this slippage is connected to the phenomenon of rigid radicalism that we discussed in our introduction and explore more deeply in the next chapter.

Chapter 4: Stifling Air, Burnout, Political Performance

Capitalism, colonialism and heteropatriarchy make us sick. Are our responses healing us? Are our actions generating wellbeing for others? Or are we unintentionally reproducing the kind of relationships that made us sick in the first place?

—Zainab Amadahy[1]

Puritanism, in whatever expression, is a poisonous germ. On the surface everything may look strong and vigorous; yet the poison works its way persistently, until the entire fabric is doomed.

—Emma Goldman[2]

Toxic contours

There is something that circulates in many radical spaces, movements, and milieus that saps their power from within. It is the pleasure of feeling more radical than others and the worry about not being radical enough; the sad comfort of sorting unfolding events into dead categories; the vigilant apprehension of errors and complicities in oneself and others; the anxious posturing on social media with the highs of being liked and the lows of being ignored; the suspicion and resentment felt in the presence of something new; the way curiosity feels naïve and condescension feels right. We can sense its emergence at certain times, when we feel the need to perform in certain ways, hate the right things, and make the right gestures. Above all, it is hostile to difference, curiosity, openness, and experimentation.

This phenomenon cannot be exhaustively described, because it is always mutating and recirculating. The problem is not simply that people are unaware of it—we think it is common among those touched by radical milieus. As the anarchist researcher and organizer Chris Dixon writes,

> Whenever this topic comes up in discussions, I've found it quickly evokes head nods and horror stories about takedowns on social media, organizational territorialism, activist social status hierarchies, sectarian posturing, and a general atmosphere of radical self-righteousness.[3]

It can be risky to discuss all this publicly; there is always the chance that one will be cast as a liberal, an oppressor, or a reactionary. For this reason, these conversations are happening between people who already trust each other enough to know that they will not be met with immediate suspicion or attack. Here there is room for questioning and listening, with space for subtlety, nuance, and care that is so often absent when rigid radicalism takes hold. These are some of the questions we have been asking in our research: What is this force? What are its contours, and what are its sources? What triggers it, and what makes it spread? How can it be warded off, and how are people activating other ways of being?

Rigid radicalism is both *a fixed way of being* and *a way of fixing*. It fixes in the sense of attempting to repair, seeing emergent movements as inherently flawed. To fix is to *see lack everywhere* and treat struggles and projects as broken and insufficient. It also fixes in the sense of fastening or making permanent, converting fluid practices into set ways of being, stagnating their transformative potential. Even though unfolding practices might appear identical to each other from a distance, habits and certainties can take over from what was once experimental and lively. When rigidity and suspicion take over, joy dies out.

This is probably our bleakest chapter, focusing as it does on the contours of rigid radicalism and how it circulates. We want to offer up some ideas about how this all works, but we are not trying to pin it down once and for all. We have been reading about this phenomenon, talking with friends, and interviewing people, and so we hope to contribute to a conversation that we know is ongoing. We want to tell stories about it, not *the* story. We do not think there is any single cause or a single response.

In our first attempts at writing about this, and in many of our interviews, we used the concept of "sad militancy" to describe this phenomenon, but we have abandoned the term because it has not worked for some people we talked with. Drawing on Spinoza's conception of sadness as stagnation, the notion of sad militancy has been circulating for a while, especially in Latin America. Nevertheless, we have noticed that it can easily be interpreted instead as a pathologization or condemnation of depression or sorrow. Furthermore we use the word "radicalism" because we want to avoid creating a dichotomy between two types of militancy. Rigid radicalism is not the "opposite" of joyful militancy; they are two different processes, animated by distinct affects.

It is a bit scary to write about these tendencies. Throughout the process of writing this book, we have come up against the worry that it will be decided we got it wrong: that we are reactionaries or liberals or oppressive in some way that we had not anticipated. Someone will reveal that we do not have "good politics," that the book is too theoretical, or not theoretical enough, or romantic, or full of hippy shit, or naïve, or misleading, or problematic, or liberal, or useless, or, or, or. We will have committed our ridiculous ideas to print, in a permanent humiliation. For us, this fear exposes the durability of rigid radicalism and how it can trigger paranoia, impose self-censorship and conformity, and encourage a kind of detached self-righteousness.

It's *those* people

These conversations are already happening frequently. Rigid radicalism is a *public secret*: something that people already sense but that nonetheless maintains its affective hold.[4] It structures desires and movements in disempowering ways despite our awareness and keeps us stuck in loops of anxiety, fear, suspicion, and certainty. As such, it cannot be attacked head-on.

When this public secret is discussed, it is all too easily converted into a moralistic argument, targeting individuals or groups: the problem is *those* rigid radicals, *out there,* separate from *us.* Some criticisms of rigid radicalism set themselves apart from or above it, as if they are the ones who truly see, and rigid radicals are trapped in a fog. The problem is that this critique repeats a common stance of rigid radicalism itself: someone holds a truth and brings it to others in need of enlightenment. We hope to approach rigid radicalism differently, while recognizing that it is easy to slip into, to stoke, and to activate.

Like joyful militancy, rigid radicalism cannot be reduced to certain people or behaviors. It is not that there are a bunch of assholes out there stifling movements and imploding worlds. In fact, this vigilant search for flawed people or behaviors—and the exposure of them everywhere—can be part of rigid radicalism itself. As a public secret, there is no point in shouting about it. It is more like a gas: continually circulating, working on us behind our backs, and guiding us towards rigidities, closures, and hostility.

No one is immune to it, just as no one is immune to being pulled into liberalism and other patterns of Empire. The air makes us cough certainties: some feel provoked and attack or shrink away; others push cough medicine; but none of this stops anyone from getting sicker. For us at least, there is no cure, no gas mask, no unitary solution. There are only openings, searches, and the collective discovery of new and old ways of moving that let in fresh air. And for the same reason that no one is immune, anyone can participate in its undoing.

To confront rigid radicalism effectively, we think, is not to pin it down and attack it but to understand it so that we can learn to dissipate it. Because these tendencies are linked to fear, anxiety, shame—to our very desires and sense of who we are and what we are becoming—we think it is important to approach all of this with care and compassion. It also requires recognizing and making the other tendencies palpable: rigid radicalism is always already coming apart, and joy is always already emerging. Ultimately, we think that rigidity is undone by activating, stoking, and intensifying joy, and defending it with militancy and gentleness; in other words, figuring out how to transform our own situations, treat each other well, listen to each other, experiment, and fight together.

The paradigm of government

Where does rigid radicalism come from? Surely there are a multiplicity of sources. Ultimately, we think it is an inheritance of Empire. It has been suggested to us that rigid radicalism is primarily a Euro-colonial phenomenon: that is, it is most intense in spaces where whiteness, heteropatriarchy, and colonization have the strongest hold.[5] These divisions induce habits of relating based in crisis and lack, as capitalism constantly pits people and groups in competition with each other. But rigid radicalism does not exactly mimic Empire; it emerges as a reaction to it, as an aspiration to be *purely against it*. When we spoke to adrienne maree brown, she suggested that it is an outgrowth of terror and violence:

NICK AND CARLA: What sustains it?

BROWN: The culture that there is only one way to be radical in the world, one way to create change.

NICK AND CARLA: What provokes or inspires it? What makes it spread?

BROWN: Terror. We are dying out here. So much destruction is in motion. I think there is a feeling of urgency, that we need discipline and rigor to meet this massive threat to our existence—racism, capitalism, climate, all of it. It feels like we need to be an army.[6]

Empire's destruction in motion can trigger desires for control and militarized discipline. It can lead to a monolithic notion of the right way to be radical, hostile, and suspicious towards other ways of being. It forces out the messiness of relationships and everyday life in favor of clear lines between good/bad and radical/reactionary. In this sense, rigid radicalism imports Empire's tendencies of *fixing, governing, disciplining, and controlling*, while presenting these as a means of liberation or revolution. In this sense, many radical movements in the West (and elsewhere) have been entangled in what Spanish intellectual Amador Fernández-Savater has called the *paradigm of government*:

> In the paradigm of government, being a militant implies always being angry with what happens, because it is not what should happen; always chastising others, because they are not aware of what they should be aware of; always frustrated, because what exists is lacking in this or that; always anxious, because the real is permanently headed in the wrong direction and you have to subdue it, direct it, straighten it. All of this implies not enjoying, never letting yourself be carried away by the situation, not trusting in the forces of the world.[7]

In the paradigm of government, one always has an idea of what *should* be happening, and this gets in the way of being present with what is *always already* happening and the capacity to be attuned to the transformative potentials in one's own situation. Under the paradigm of government, people are never committed enough. Silvia Federici spoke to this when we interviewed her:

This is why I don't believe in the concept of "self-sacrifice," where self-sacrifice means that we do things that go against our needs, our desires, our potentials, and for the sake of political work we have to repress ourselves. This has been a common practice in political movements in the past. But it is one that produces constantly dissatisfied individuals.[8]

Because rigid radicalism induces a sense of duty and obligation everywhere, there is a constant sense that one is never doing enough. In this context, burnout in radical spaces is not just about being worn out by hard work; it is often code for being wounded, depleted, and frayed: *"I'm fucking burning."* What depletes us is not just long hours but also the tendencies of shame, anxiety, mistrust, competition, and perfectionism. It is the way in which these tendencies stifle joy: they prevent the capacity for collective creativity, experimentation, and transformation. Often, saying one is burned out is the safest way to disappear, to take a break, to take care of oneself and get away from these dynamics.

Decline and counterrevolution

Rigid radicalism often arises as a reaction to a decline of transformative and enabling movements. Empire, for its part, responds to resurgent movements and uprisings by deploying ever more sophisticated forms of repression and control. Surveillance, criminalization, and imprisonment are used to destroy people's capacity to organize. Waves of austerity and accumulation lead to more debt, higher costs of living, and economic scarcity. Pacification through the NGO-industrial complex helps to capture and domesticate movements so that they can be managed and organizing can be professionalized. This is always at least partially effective: parts of movements get destroyed, co-opted, subdued, and divided. In the process, what was once a transformative practice can become a stagnant ritual, emptied of its power. Sebastian Touza gives an example from his experience in the student movement in Argentina:

> I think shifts toward joy often happen when people organize to do things in novel ways because there is a new opportunity to organize or because the old ways no longer work. I became a member of the student movement at my university at the end of the last dictatorship in Argentina in 1983. I remember the first years of consolidation of the democratic institutions as a period in which experimentation was alive. The people of my generation had no idea what a political party was like (after eight years of dictatorship during which parties were prohibited). Militants were willing to revise everything, were open to listen to all sorts of ideas about how to organize. Today, as a professor, two or three generations of student militants later, I see the students at the university where I work too convinced that doing things the way they do them is the only possible way. All ideas about politics as experimentation have been lost in the student movement, if we can call a movement a collection of people who rarely think outside their respective party lines. Joy has to do with a capacity for new encounters, to a disposition to new affects and ideas, with desiring differently, with setting into question the reproduction of things as they are. Sadness, on the contrary,

has to do with fear of leaving the safety of a routine which lets many survive but very few or nobody at all to really live and enjoy what they do.[9]

In times of decline there is a tendency for movements to turn inward or fixate on old strategies or received ways of doing things. Curiosity calcifies into certainty, closing off the capacity for experimentation along with its transformative potential.

The perils of comparing

Rigid radicalism can also take hold through comparing one's own situation with other times and places. From a certain perspective, it can be depressing to hear about places where the social fabric is much stronger, where there are deep traditions of mutual aid, or where struggles against Empire are visible, widespread, and intense. It can activate a feeling that people around us are too flawed, too complacent, or that our own worlds are lacking something: that they are not insurrectionary enough, not big enough, not militant enough, not caring enough. Change can feel out of reach across an unbridgeable chasm. This can lead to cynicism and pessimism and a detached certainty that the here and now is not a place of joy and transformation: *revolts might be widespread elsewhere, but everything is fucked here; people are passive, and there is no real struggle going on.*

Alternatively, the chasm can lead to a desire to cultivate only one's own garden or retreat into little cliques and milieus, where there is a semblance of safety, security, and predictability: *everything around us is corrupt, but we can live out our beautiful ideals in our own little world.* This is the creation of alternatives in isolation rather than through combat that connects to other movements and forms of life.

It can also lead to the endless refinement of a militant ideology that provides certainty to its adherents, continually reinforced by the perceived failures of those who do things differently: *if they only understood, in the way that we do, things would be different.* These cynical, escapist, or ideological responses to Empire are completely understandable. We feel this way often. We have noticed that it happens, in particular, when we anxiously evaluate our own lives or situations in relation to others, against a universal standard of radicalness.

Having good politics

> But enough! Enough! I can't endure it any more. Bad air! Bad air! This workshop where man fabricates ideals—it seems to me it stinks from nothing but lies.
> —Friedrich Nietzsche[10]

One way we see this measuring stick of radicalness materializing is through the notion of "good politics." In many places today, it has become common to say of an individual or group, "they have good politics." What does it mean to *have* good politics? What happens when politics becomes something a person *has*, rather than something people *do together*, as a shared practice? What happens when shared practices always have to be announced and their goodness displayed? Increasingly, we suggest, having good politics means taking the right positions, saying the right things, circulating the most radical things on Facebook or Twitter or Tumblr, calling out the right people for being wrong, and having well-formed opinions. In this sense, having good politics is similar to "having a good analysis." When analysis becomes a trait, rather than a collective and curious process, it stagnates.

We are encouraged—and we often encourage each other—to wear our politics and analysis like badges, as markers of distinction. When politics becomes something that one *has*, like fashion, it always needs to be visible in order to function. Actions need to be publicized, positions need to be taken, and our everyday lives need to be spoken loudly to each other. One is encouraged to make calculations about political commitments based on how they will be seen and by whom. Politics becomes a spectacle to be performed. This reaches its height online, where sharing the right things and speaking the right words tend to be *the only* ways that people can know each other. Groups need to turn inward and constantly evaluate themselves in relation to these ideals and then project them outward, proclaiming their intentions, values, programs, and missions.

But since one can only *have* good politics in comparison to someone else that lacks them, rigid radicalism tends towards constant comparison and measuring. Often the best way to avoid humiliation for lacking good politics is to find *others* lacking in militancy, radicalism, anti-oppression, or some other ideal. One's politics can never quite match these perfectionist ideals, so one is subjected to constant shame and fear.

When radicals attack each other in the game of good politics, it is due at least in part to the fact that *this is a place where people can exercise some power*. Even if one is unable to challenge capitalism and white supremacy as structures or to participate in transformative struggles, one can always attack *others* for being complicit with Empire and tell oneself that these attacks are radical in and of themselves. One's opponents in the game of good politics and rigid radicalism are not capitalists or white supremacists or police; they are others vying for the *correct ways* of thinking about and fighting capitalism, white supremacy, and policing. Comparison and evaluation of different camps or currents can be so constant that they become an end in itself: every encounter with a new current must be approached with a distrustful search for flaws. We come to know others— their beliefs, their commitments, their worth—based on how good they are at staking out a position.

In this sense, rigid radicalism is not one political current but a tendency that seeps into many different currents and milieus today. In some milieus, the currency of good politics is a stated (or demonstrated) willingness for direct action, riots, property destruction, and clashes with police. In others, it is the capacity for anti-oppressive analysis, avoidance of oppressive statements, and the calling out of those who make them. In others it is the capacity to avoid work and survive without buying things or paying rent. In some it is adherence to a vision of leftism or revolution, and in others it is the conviction that the Left is dead and revolution is a stupid fantasy. In some it is the capacity to have participated in a lot of projects or to be connected to a big network of radical organizers. In every case, there is a tendency for one milieu to dismiss the commitments and values of the others and to expose their inadequacies. At its extreme, this generates a form of sectarianism that is fueled by the very act of being vocally sectarian.

The newcomer is immediately placed in a position of debt: owing dedication, self-sacrifice, and correct analysis that must be continuously proved. Whether it is the performance of anti-oppressive language, revolutionary fervor, nihilist detachment, or an implicit dress code, those who are unfamiliar with the expectations of the milieu are doomed from the start unless they "catch up" and conform. In subtle and overt ways, they will be attacked, mocked, and excluded for getting it wrong, even though these people are often the ones that "good politics" is supposed to support: those without formal education who have not been exposed much to radical milieus, but who have a stake in fighting.

None of this is meant to suggest that we should be more wishy-washy about oppression, or that hard lines are wrong, or that all radical practices are corrupt or bad. Developing analysis, naming mistakes, and engaging in conflict are all indispensable. To undo rigid radicalism is not a call to "get along" or "shut up and take action" or "be spontaneous." People's capacities to challenge and unlearn oppressive behaviors, take direct action, or avoid selling labor and paying rent can create and deepen cracks in Empire. They can all be part of joyful transformation. But any of these practices can also become measuring sticks for comparison and evaluation that end up devaluing other practices and stifling the growth of collective capacities.

When politics circulates in a world dominated by hypervisibility and rigidity, there is a huge swath of things that do not count and can never count: the incredible things that people do when nobody is looking, the ways that people support and care for each other quietly and without recognition, the hesitations and stammerings that come through the encounter with other ways of living and fighting, all the acts of resistance and sabotage that remain secret, the slow transformations that take years or decades, and all of the ineffable, joyful movements and struggles that can never be fully captured in words or displayed publicly. Rigid radicalism is a barrier to co-learning, listening, and questioning, and to undoing our subjection (our sedimented habits). It blocks the difficult recovery and discovery of responsibility and the capacity to carve out relationships based in trust and care. The game of good politics makes it much more difficult to be humble, responsive, and creative. No one can *have* any of this. Joyful common notions can never be possessed; they can only be developed and sustained collectively. They are shared powers that grow in and through transformative relationships and struggles. When held up as a badge of honor or gripped as an identity, they die, detached from the processes and relationships that animate them.

Rigid radicalism stifles joy: it drains out vital energies by enforcing external norms and standards and by feeding insecurities and anxieties. The greatest tragedy of all is that it does so by converting a lived and changing radicalism into a stifling *ideal,* like a horizon that is always in view, distant and receding.

These tendencies have led many to abandon radical milieus. This is the narrowing of possibilities induced by rigid radicalism: either continue in a stifling and depleting atmosphere, or leave and attempt to live the form of life that is offered up by Empire. For many, this is not a choice at all because one's very survival is connected to the same spaces where rigid radicalism has taken hold. In this sense, rigid radicalism can be lethal. At the same time, efforts to transform all this are already underway, and many people are initiating conversations about undoing some of these tendencies within the milieus they inhabit. Others are fleeing explicitly radical milieus, creating something new at the margins of both Empire and visibly radical spaces. By breaking off with a crew of friends, some have built quieter alternatives and hubs elsewhere that enable new forms of movement and revive squelched possibilities. There are many ways of letting in fresh air. Rigid radicalism is *only one tendency among others*, even when it is the dominant one. This is why we have started with—and focused on—joyful militancy in this book.

Chapter 5: Undoing Rigid Radicalism, Activating Joy

How does one keep from being fascist, even (especially) when one believes oneself to be a revolutionary militant? How do we rid our speech and our acts, our hearts and our pleasures, of fascism? How do we ferret out the fascism that is ingrained in our behavior?
—Michel Foucault[1]

Three stories of rigid radicalism

We want to share three stories about some of the origins of rigid radicalism, along with the ways it is constantly being undone through people's capacity for joy and the formulation of common notions. We focus on three overlapping sources: ideology, morality, and paranoid reading.

The story of ideology begins in currents of Marxism-Leninism that have animated movements throughout the twentieth century. But the problem is broader than Leninist vanguardism—it is ideology as such, and the ways that ideological thinking nurtures fixed answers, certainties, and sectarianism. In any movement, ideological rigidity is only one tendency among others, and it is being challenged by currents that are relatively *non-ideological*. Whether explicit or not, non-ideological ways of moving and relating recover space for experimentation, and they tend to privilege relationships and feeling over dogmatic principles.

A second story begins with Christian morality and its penchants for creating sinners and saints and for inducing guilt and fear. Rigid radicalism is stoked by a moralism that attempts to root out any shred of complicity with Empire, and in the process it often erases complexity and animates self-righteousness. At the same time, people are undoing this in a multiplicity of ways, including through ethical attunement to their own situations and by making space for all kinds of responses that escape the grip of moralism.

Finally, the story of paranoid reading is traced back to schooling and the way that students are taught to internalize constant evaluation. Detached from the immediacy of life, measuring everything in relation to fixed standards, it becomes possible to find inadequacies everywhere. When these tendencies take over, there is no space for celebration or surprise. At the same time, we point to some of the ways that this is being undone, not by abandoning critique but by recovering complementary capacities to explore potential and encounter new things.

Ideology

The militant diagram

Either you respect people's capacities to think for
themselves, to govern themselves, to creatively devise
their own best ways to make decisions, to be accountable, to relate, problem-solve, break-down isolation and
commune in a thousand different ways ... OR: you dis-
respect them. You dis-respect ALL of us.

—Ashanti Alston[2]

A major force that has contributed to rigid radicalism is
rigid ideology and its tendency to generate certainties and
fixed answers that close off the potential for experimentation. Alongside the Marxist critique of capitalist ideology
was an aspiration to replace it with a *revolutionary anti-
capitalist* ideology. It was thought that revolution required
a unified consciousness among proletarians: they needed to
be taught that it was in their interests to overthrow capitalism. The revolutionary vanguard was tasked with developing and disseminating this ideology, and with everything
in life subordinated to the goal of revolution, everyone and
everything could be treated instrumentally, as a means to
the seizure of state power and the end of capitalism.

The philosopher Nick Thoburn links this revolutionary anti-capitalist ideology to what he calls a "militant
diagram": a persistent affective and ideological tendency
that first emerged through Bolshevism and Leninism.[3] It

was later expressed in movements throughout the twentieth century, from Third World national liberation struggles to socialist formations in North America and Europe to Black Power in the 1960s and '70s. According to Colectivo Situaciones, a militant research group in Argentina, this figure of militancy is always "setting out the party line,"

> keeping for himself a knowledge of what ought to happen in the situation, which he always approaches from outside, in an instrumental and transitive way (situations have value as moments of a general strategy that encompasses them), because his fidelity is, above all, ideological and preexists all situations.[4]

The notion of a correct party line took different forms among different movements, but the basic (hierarchical, rigid) structure was the same: a certain privileged group would help usher in the revolution through a correct interpretation of theory and the unfolding of history. Despite joyful transformations and insurrectionary openings, tendencies towards vanguardism and rigid ideology often led groups towards isolation and stagnation.

Among many other groups, these tendencies can be seen in the US-based Weather Underground, a militant white anti-imperialist group active during the 1970s. They are best-known for their series of bombings targeting public infrastructure and monuments, conducted in an attempt to wake up white Americans to realities of US imperialism such as the government's slaughter of Vietnamese people and its assassination of Black Panthers.

They also adopted Maoist self-criticism in order to ferret out any trace of the dominant ideology within their group. Criticism sessions, which could last for hours or even days, involved members discussing weaknesses, tactical mistakes, emotional investments, preparedness for violence, and even sexual proclivities in an effort to shed all attachments to the dominant order and induce a revolutionary way of being.[5] Even the most ruthless criticism could be justified as part of this process, and the Weather Underground developed a whole regimen of practices designed to purify themselves of any trace of dominant ideology, coupled with constant injunctions towards (what they saw as) the most militant forms of action possible.

While their tactics were controversial, they were also widely supported at the time, and the Weather Underground was only one of many groups that were bombing and sabotaging corporate and government infrastructure. What we are interested in getting at is not particular tactics, nor something specific to underground groups, but the way that certain tendencies of thought, action, and feeling can congeal into stifling patterns. As former Weather Underground member Bernardine Dohrn writes,

> Weather succumbed to dogma, arrogance, and certainty. We were not alone. There was recovery, and amends that are still underway. But the perceived necessity to have answers to everything and to struggle endlessly resulted in ungenerous and damaging leadership, harm to great comrades, and wretched behavior.[6]

As Bill Ayers, another former member, explains, the attempt to escape completely from a culture of white supremacy and capitalist conformity enforced an intense, alternative orthodoxy:

> It was fanatical obedience, we militant nonconformists suddenly tripping over one another to be exactly alike, following the sticky roles of congealed idealism. I cannot reproduce the stifling atmosphere that overpowered us. Events came together with the gentleness of an impending train wreck, and there was the sad sensation of waiting for impact.[7]

Though the goal was to create revolutionary forms of organization capable of overthrowing the US government, their ideological rigidity and norms of relentless self-sacrifice paradoxically isolated them further and further from the "masses" that they sought to mobilize.

When we interviewed him, Gustavo Esteva discussed his own experience of Marxist-Leninist militancy in Latin America during this time:

> In the '60s, when I became associated with a group in the process of organizing a guerrilla group in Mexico, whose members were assuming that they were already the vanguard of the proletariat because they had the revolutionary program, I was fully immersed in what we now call sad militancy. Our "program" was evidently an intellectual

construction in the Leninist tradition. We had already our criticism of Stalinism, et cetera, but we still were in the tradition of trying to seize the power of the state for a revolution from the top down, through social engineering. We were thus preparing ourselves (military training, etc.) and organizing. Of course, there were moments or conditions of joy, laughter, intensified emotion, exhilaration.... The environment of conspiracy and clandestinity and the shared ideology shaped real camaraderie and episodes full of joy, but it was clear that the experience itself was pure sad militancy, full of creating boundaries, making distinctions, comparing, making plans, and so on.... How the whole experience ended makes the point better than any of those stories: one of our leaders killed the other leader because of a woman. The episode evidenced for us the kind of violence we were accumulating in ourselves and wanted to impose on the whole society. In the military training, for an army or a guerrilla, to learn how to use a weapon is pretty easy; what is difficult is to learn to kill someone in cold blood, someone like you, that did nothing personal against you.... Nothing sadder than that.[8]

The experience of the Weather Underground and Esteva both make it clear that these ideological tendencies are not just about ideas; they also contain their own pleasures and highs, induced in part by the sense of being clandestine and more aware than "the masses." Ideology is not simply rigid and cold: it can include a warm sense of belonging and camaraderie among its adherents.

This tendency has percolated into contemporary movements and groups, including those that are not directly influenced by Marxism-Leninism or Maoism. Nick Thoburn suggests,

> It is a central paradox of militancy that as an organization constitutes itself as a unified body it tends to become closed to the outside, to the non-militant, those who would be the basis of any mass movement. Indeed, to the degree that the militant body conceives of itself as having discovered the correct revolutionary principle and establishes its centre of activity on adherence to this principle, it has a tendency to develop hostility to those who fall short of its standard.[9]

As militant rigidity increases, a gap widens between the group and its outside. But a single, unified Marxism-Leninism has existed only as a dream. In reality, there has been a proliferation of sectarian commitments to various ideologies, including strains of Marxism, anarchism, socialism, and so on. Ideological thinking is not necessarily something escaped through more and better thinking. For Esteva, one of the things that fundamentally destabilized the strictures of his Leninism was his joyful encounter with others and their confidence in their own capacities to respond to problems with conviviality:

The joy of living, the passion for fiestas, the capacity to express emotions, the social climate that I found at the grassroots, in villages and barrios, in the midst of extreme misery, began to change my attitudes. My participation in different kinds of peasant and urban marginal movements gave me a radically different approach. The break point was perhaps the explosion of autonomy and self-organization after the earthquake in Mexico City in 1985. It became for me a life-changing experience. The victims of the earthquake were suffering all kinds of hardships. They had lost friends and relatives, their homes, their possessions, almost everything. Their convivial reconstruction of their lives and culture would not have been possible without the amazing passion for living they showed at every moment. Such passion had very powerful political expressions and was the seed for amazing social movements. In the following years the balance of forces changed in Mexico City, already a monstrous settlement of fifteen million people. There was a radical contrast between the guerrilla and these movements. The very notion of militancy changed in me: it was no longer associated with an organization, a party, an ideology, and even less a war.... It was an act of love.[10]

To experience joy in this way is not simply to feel good but also to be transformed. Esteva's experience with the grassroots led him to center conviviality and joy in his work and his life while continuing to be involved with and support militant movements, including the Zapatistas and the insurrectionary uprisings in Oaxaca.

For us, this shows that militancy is always about more than tactics or combativeness; it is tied to questions of affect: how movements enable people to grow their own capacities and become new people (or don't). Marina Sitrin consistently foregrounds affect in her own work with horizontalist movements in Argentina, and when we interviewed her for this book, she talked about her experience with the different affective spaces created by groups she has been involved with:

> On a basic level, the space a group or movement creates from the beginning is key—the tone and openness, or not, makes a big difference if one wants to focus on new relationships with one another. Along these same lines, ideological rigidity and hierarchies in ideas, formal and informal, create a closed and eventually nasty space for those not ascribing to the ideology or a part of the clique. People do not stay in movements that organize in this way, or if they do it is with a sort of obedience that is not transformative and instead creates versions of the same power and hierarchy....
>
> My early organizing experiences were fortunately with anti-racist and later Central American solidarity movements, with people who had been a part of the civil rights and later anti-nuclear movements, so who had a focus at least in part on social

relationships and democracy. Later, however, when I decided I needed to be a part of a revolutionary group that was organizing against capitalism as a whole, well, I found myself in a few different centrist socialist groups which were really soul-deadening. It was all about ideology and guilt. One could never do enough and could never know enough or quote enough of whomever was the revolutionary of the day (James Cannon, Tony Cliff, etc.). It was also politically all about the end and not the day-to-day, that even included women, which one would think, after the radical feminist movement, [that] these groups would get that relationships have to change now; but, no, it was all about the future free society we all had to work for—accepting relationships as they are, pretty much.

I later came around some anarchist groups, thinking that they would be more open and focused on the day-to-day, as that is what I had read from the theory, but found the rigidity around identity too harsh, and since I was not squatting or dressing a certain way I was kept at arm's length—which was fine since I felt too rejected to try very hard.[11]

Sitrin's account makes it clear that rigid radicalism does not stem from one ideology or group in particular. Marxism-Leninism has lost its grip on many movements, and accounts of such groups can sound strange and distant today. In North America, at least, the dream of a revolutionary seizure of state power has lost a lot of its force, but in many cases Marxist ideology has been superseded by other ideological closures and sectarian tendencies. Currents of anarchism can be just as hostile and ideologically rigid.

Ideology in anarchism

Anarchism is a vibrant and complex tradition. At their most joyful, anarchist currents support common notions such as mutual aid, autonomy, direct action, and solidarity while refusing ideological closures. At the same time, however, anarchists have always grappled with ideology. The early twentieth-century anarchist feminist Emma Goldman shared this experience in her autobiography:

> At the dances I was one of the most untiring and gayest. One evening a cousin of Sasha [Alexander Berkman], a young boy, took me aside. With a grave face, as if he were about to announce the death of a dear comrade, he whispered to me that it did not behoove an agitator to dance. Certainly not with such reckless abandon, anyway. It was undignified for one who was on the way to become a force in the anarchist movement. My frivolity would only hurt the Cause.
>
> I grew furious at the impudent interference of the boy. I told him to mind his own business, I was tired of having the Cause constantly thrown into my face. I did not believe that a Cause which stood for a beautiful ideal, for anarchism, for release and freedom from conventions and prejudice, should demand the denial of life and joy. I insisted that

our Cause could not expect me to become a nun
and that the movement should not be turned into
a cloister. If it meant that, I did not want it. "I want
freedom, the right to self-expression, everybody's
right to beautiful, radiant things." Anarchism
meant that to me, and I would live it in spite of the
whole world–prisons, persecution, everything. Yes,
even in spite of the condemnation of my own comrades I would live my beautiful ideal.[12]

Since Goldman wrote about this a century ago, this
kind of policing has continued in new and different ways.
While Maoism and Leninism were ascendant in radical
politics, it took the form of maintaining an explicit party
line. With the decline of these ideologies, rigid radicalism has shape-shifted into new forms. One of the ideological tendencies animating anarchist and anti-authoritarian
spaces is what Amory Starr calls "grumpywarriorcool."
Rather than the militant conformity of Marxist-Leninism,
grumpywarriorcool manifests as an ideology of individualistic *anti-conformity and anti-vanguardism*. Starr gives a
polemical example of the "manarchist" whose "freedom" to
do whatever he wants ends up reinforcing individualism,
whiteness, and patriarchy:

i'm going to stink, i'm going in there even though
i'm contagious, i'm going to bring my barking dog,
i have the right to do whatever the fuck i want and
people just have to deal with it and i'm going to call
this "cultural diversity" ... meanwhile other folks

around are feeling like another white guy is doing
whatever the fuck he wants.[13]

She suggests that privileging individual freedom is ideological because it tends to force out potentials for connection,
curiosity, and a sense of collective responsibility. In Starr's
analysis, there are some continuities between grumpywarriorcool and earlier ideological forms; norms of fearlessness,
self-sacrifice, and bravery, she argues, can end up eliminating
space to express hesitation or fear. These intimate reflections
can be transformative, but they remain hidden because it is
too difficult to voice them in a climate where fearlessness is
the ideal. Similarly, Starr names "smart radicalism" as a fundamental premise of white, anti-authoritarian organizing of
grumpywarriorcool: a commitment to radical principles and
theories, a "correct" interpretation of them, and the assumption that this correctness will avoid mistakes. Forced out by
these tendencies are friendliness, comfort, generosity, and curiosity.[14] Outsiders are viewed with cool suspicion.

These stories are not meant as a criticism of anarchism
(or Marxism) as a whole; we are trying to locate ideological
tendencies within these complex and varied traditions. At
its best, anarchism has enabled the refusal of fixed ideologies in favor of experimentation, openness, autonomy, and
a proliferation of different struggles and forms of life. As
scott crow writes,

An abundance of literature has been written about
anarchism over the last hundred years. How is
it organized? What could it look like? What are

examples of it in practice? There are also complex critiques and analyses of it, but, for me, anarchism is just a point of reference, a descriptive word to get one's bearings for starting conversations that move to action. It describes an opening up of possibilities for changing ourselves and our communities. It describes a set of guiding principles and ideas, serious and playful at once, not a rigid ideology.[15]

We think this conception of anarchism—as a point of reference and an evolving set of questions—can help ward off the crystallization of fixed ideology. crow further suggests that anarchism is animated by a trust in people's ability to solve their own problems and take collective responsibility rather than a prescription for how they should do it. This is the kind of anarchism we are after: a non-ideological sensibility that nurtures trust in people's capacity to care for each other and to be responsive, inventive, and militant.

The limits of ideology

In this sense, Ashanti Alston suggests that the problem is not about displacing Marxism-Leninism or Maoism with an anarchist ideology; the problem is *ideology as such* and all the baggage that comes with it:

Ideology ... comes out of having a set of answers for something. So even for me with my anarchism, I don't think it's classical. I don't call myself an anarcho-communist or any of the others. There's definitely anarchism that's open to being in tune with

always-changing realities. For me, anarcho-commu-
nists got good points about certain things, primi-
tivists have good points about certain things. Them
two don't get along, but I get something from both
of them. I like some aspects of anarcho-individu-
alism and Tolstoy's spiritualism. For most of my
folks, my people are Christians or Muslims and
increasingly Yoruba, Kemetic, and other African
religions that they're recovering and using. I don't
want to be categorized as a particular school because I know if I do, the world I would hope to be
created won't have room for all kinds of tendencies
of anarchism, or all kinds of tendencies of people
living their lives according to their own terms.[16]

From this perspective, ideology is a screen that limits
the possibility of open-ended encounters where mutual
learning and transformation can take place. Its inducement
of conformity tends towards closed, stagnant little enclaves.
Ideological and sectarian tendencies offer the comfort of
being able to pin things down, the pleasure of feeling that
one is above or ahead of others, and the somber ability to
sort new encounters into neat categories so that one is never too unsettled or affected by anything.

Undoing ideology

Rather than becoming rooted in a single ideological current, Alston points to the potential of affirming the most

enabling parts of a multiplicity of currents. Similarly, when we interviewed Richard Day, he made a distinction between an ideological approach and an *ethical* one, like Alston's:

DAY: If someone is working ideologically, they will have a pat answer to any question that might be asked, without having to do much in the way of thinking or analysis. If you ask a liberal about smashing bank windows in a protest, they will probably say it's violent and bad; if you ask an anarchist, they will probably say it's not violence, it's destruction of stolen property and quite a valid thing to do. This is similar to working morally, in that you need only consult a tablet, ask a functionary such as a priest, and they will tell you what to do and not do.

In a critical, analytic—ethical—way of relating, it is impossible to know what one might think or feel ahead of time; that will be contingent upon many circumstances of the situation. There is likely to be much more complexity, much more nuance, less dogmatism, certainty, and purity.

In general, I think it's safe to associate ideological ways of relating with rigid radicalism, and that's why you find that so many people, all over the world, who are actually involved in the most powerful social movements and up-heavals, tend to steer away from ideology and orient more to shared values, practices, and goals.

NICK & CARLA: And not being ideological means being uncertain, as well, right?

DAY: Yeah. Working non-ideologically definitely involves an element of openness, a vulnerability, not only at the level of emotion, but also at the level of thought and of political relationships. There is a certain sort of safety in having an answer for everything.[17]

As we insisted earlier, ethics here does not mean an individualized set of fixed principles (as in consumer ethics or personal ethics) but instead a capacity to be attuned to the situation, to be immersed in it, and to create something emergent out of the existing conditions. Alston speaks to the power and potential of working across difference in ways that respect where people are coming from:

> Different consciousnesses can come from different places ... and we can figure out the dialogue, how to create a way forward that respects us all, that respects the different worlds that we come from. So for me, if that had happened back then in 1970, where would we have been right now? And for me, that's such a better way to go, 'cause for the queer community, or the Yoruba community that may exist in Brooklyn, what's best for them? Whether one is a small geographical community or tied to their ethnicity or dealing with a lifestyle, we should just be open to come together and see how we can do this in a different kind of way. That's the challenge.[18]

This is the ethics of encounter. Instead of asking whether we (or they) are inherently radical, revolutionary, or anarchist, an ethical approach asks questions about how we affect each other, what new encounters become possible, and what we can do together. None of the answers to these questions can be known in advance. They can only be asked as part of an open-ended, unfolding experiment, as markers in an always-changing world, in which we figure things out along the way. As the anarchist collective Crimethinc writes,

> If the hallmark of ideology is that it begins from an answer or a conceptual framework and attempts to work backward from there, then one way to resist ideology is to start from questions rather than answers. That is to say—when we intervene in social conflicts, doing so in order to assert *questions* rather than conclusions.
>
> What is it that brings together and defines a movement, if not questions? Answers can alienate or stupefy, but questions *seduce.* Once enamored of a question, people will fight their whole lives to answer it. Questions precede answers and outlast them: every answer only perpetuates the question that begot it.[19]

We would add that an important complement to asking questions is being able to listen sincerely to responses and to those with altogether different questions. The power of questions comes from people being able to respond and hear each other in new ways. It comes from hanging on to the uncertainties they generate and the new potential that comes along with them. To undo ideology is not as straightforward as taking off a pair of glasses to see the world differently. To ward off ideology is not finally to see clearly but to be *disoriented*, allowing things to emerge in their murkiness and complexity. It might mean seeing and feeling more but often *vaguely,* like flickers in one's peripheral vision or strange sensations that defy familiar categories and emotions. It is an undoing of oneself, cutting across the grain of habits and attachments. To step out of an inherited ideology can be joyful *and painful.*

Morality, fear, and ethical attunement

The Christian origins of morality

There is perhaps no phenomenon which contains so much destructive feeling as moral indignation, which permits envy or hate to be acted out under the guise of virtue.

—Erich Fromm[20]

There is a second story, related and overlapping but distinct: rigid radicalism can be traced to a Christian current of moralism, with its penchants for fear and hostility to a sinful world. Even within Christianity, this was not the only current; it has always also been a site of transformation and revolt.[21] But the dominant form of Christianity over centuries in Europe was a colonizing force, seeking to crush its own rebellious currents within and to convert or annihilate the rest of the world. To be successful, the Church did not merely command obedience. Through practices like confession, it taught its subjects to internalize their own sinfulness, guilt, and inadequacy. This Christian subjectivity is one based in resentment of excess and transformation, bent on spreading guilt and shame. Inspired in part by his reading of Spinoza, Friedrich Nietzsche showed how Christian morality sacralized meekness and submission, turning powerlessness into a mark of blessedness.[22] His concept of *ressentiment* names the nurturance of a deep-seated hatred and fear of otherness, *and* of one's own sinful desires, based in a stultifying morality.

Over the last several centuries guilt and shame have undergone a secular conversion, rejecting the Church for its superstition, while embracing *ressentiment*. This secular subject hates the Church but loves its poison.[23] The affective structures of *lack, guilt, fear, and purism* remains intact.

Morality in movement

Don't be in such a hurry to condemn a person because he doesn't do what you do, or think as you think or as fast. There was a time when you didn't know what you know today.

—Malcolm X[24]

Liberal morality seeps into movements in the form of incessant regulation and pacification of struggles. It replaces the transformative power of dignity with moral indignation and its tendencies of shame and self-righteousness. It pathologizes anger, hatred, and destruction, turning non-violence into a moral imperative rather than a tactic. This is the morality of the cop who tells you to calm down with one hand on his gun; the sympathizer whose "support" for you evaporates as soon as things become "violent"; the citizen who says you had better vote or you can't complain. People in struggle are constantly told about the "correct" way of conducting themselves if they want to be respected and heard. The liberal morality of whiteness converts racism and sexism into matters of individual prejudice. Conversations about violence and oppression are constantly derailed by individual emotions and the erasure of power relations where white feelings matter more than Black lives.

Under the stifling weight of liberal morality, *anti-liberal* morality has grown in reaction. The targets and the enemies change, but the structure remains, and radical morality can reach new heights of corrosive self-righteousness and punishment. From this perspective, things are always in danger of becoming infected or diluted by liberalism. Liberal or oppressive sentiments must be attacked wherever they are detected. Call-outs and radical takedowns proliferate. Indignation grows: everything is corrupt and tainted; nothing is as it should be. This "as it should be" is no longer determined by Christian priests or politicians and good citizens but by a *radical* certainty that one is on the right side of a moral drama between good and evil.

Like the old Christian morality, new forms of moralism subsist on the evils they decry: to remain pious, the priest must reveal new sins. This can surface as an incessant search for oppression and a ceaseless attack on anyone who is found guilty, including oneself, through new forms of confession, trials, and punishments. The new Other is the not-radical-enough, the liberal, the perpetrator, the oppressor.

A number of our interlocutors have pointed out how these moralistic tendencies towards punishment can end up excluding many of those who are supposed to be centered by anti-oppressive practices: poor people, people without formal education, and others who haven't been exposed to the ever evolving language of radical communities. In a compassionate way, Kelsey Cham C. shares their experience with call-out culture and language policing upon being introduced to radical communities:

> When I came out as queer in Montreal ... I started to find accurate words to describe how I felt about the world. Even though this skill was my entry into more political communities, I still felt incredibly judged. It was like an ultra-heightened experience of not being allowed in the cool-kid club in high school—but with all new rules that I had not learned and that no one took the time to explain to me. The language I grew up with could no longer be applied and would sometimes get me kicked out of social settings. My entire experience of growing up was judged and I felt totally isolated in trying to figure out why.
>
> As I've gotten older, I've figured out the "right way" to navigate in these communities by learning language protocol and radical terminology while

dropping the offensive and oppressive slang. I don't disagree with changing language to support systems we care about. I do disagree with judging people for not knowing the rules—especially since radicals are often organizing in favor of marginalized communities who are generally not aware of these rules.

If I wanted to fill out a form to describe my identity, I could check a bunch of boxes that would make my experience worth standing up for: Queer. Trans. Person of Color. Former Sex Trade Worker. Ironically, the biggest advocates for people like me—the people ready to throw down stats about harm reduction and youth, gender queer folks, and the vulnerable people in society—many of them had no patience for me. I came into their communities looking for support, friends, and direction. I came having left abusive and sexually manipulative partners. I came in hella lost, unaware, and not very educated. But I came in agreement with their political perspectives, because I knew society was fucked from the time I was twelve—maybe even younger. In high school, while other kids wrote about teen heartbreak, I wrote about injustices I saw everywhere. I came into these radical communities wanting to make change, but all my habits and the language I had learned to protect myself with got me in shit.[25]

Cham C.'s story gets at a common experience in radical milieus, in which language and conduct are intensely scrutinized, and those who fail are often forced out. Far from arbitrary, these rules are often earnest attempts to root out oppressive behaviors, with the aspiration of creating spaces where everyday habits and language are less laden with structural violence. In a world where white supremacy, homophobia, transphobia, misogyny, and other forms of violence are incessant, the desire to create spaces that feel a little safer makes a lot of sense. Yet, as Cham C. explains, they can become stifling and exclusionary in the enforcement of a "right" way of being.

What reinforces rigid radicalism, we think, is not the attempt to change language or behavior but the way these attempts can be subsumed by moralism and reinforce shame, blame, punishment, and guilt. Morality is dangerous not only because it can reinforce oppression but also because it can divorce people from their own power. People are reduced to their statements, becoming symptoms or examples of violence rather than complex and changing beings. Moral indignation can promote stagnation, encouraging complaints and condemnations that lead nowhere. The desire to be morally right can get in the way of here-and-now transformation.

Warding off morality with common notions

Squeezed out by morality, we think, are *common notions*: ethical, responsive ways of relating that are tuned to the complexities of each situation and capable of supporting collective transformation. When morality takes over, common notions are converted into rigid principles or practices that can no longer be questioned. This can be seen

in what has become known as "call-out culture" in many
radical milieus: the prevalence of publicly attacking certain
statements or behaviors as oppressive. As Toronto-based
writer Asam Ahmad writes,

> What makes call-out culture so toxic is not neces-
> sarily its frequency so much as the nature and per-
> formance of the call-out itself. Especially in online
> venues like Twitter and Facebook, calling someone
> out isn't just a private interaction between two indi-
> viduals: it's a public performance where people can
> demonstrate their wit or how pure their politics
> are. Indeed, sometimes it can feel like the perfor-
> mance itself is more significant than the content of
> the call-out.
>
> Call-out culture can end up mirroring what the
> prison industrial complex teaches us about crime
> and punishment: to banish and dispose of individu-
> als rather than to engage with them as people with
> complicated stories and histories.
>
> It isn't an exaggeration to say that there is a mild
> totalitarian undercurrent not just in call-out culture
> but also in how progressive communities police
> and define the bounds of who's in and who's out.
> More often than not, this boundary is constructed
> through the use of appropriate language and ter-
> minology – a language and terminology that are
> forever shifting and almost impossible to keep up
> with. In such a context, it is impossible not to fail at
> least some of the time.[26]

Through its toxic performance, call-out culture can activate and intensify a climate of fear, shame, and self-righteousness. It is important to note that none of the voices we are bringing into this chapter are suggesting that calling people out, naming oppression, or creating boundaries is wrong. Because oppression is so pervasive and people's responses to it are so heavily policed and pathologized, these can be hard conversations to have. We want to suggest that this conversation is already being had in ways that are more open, transformative, and *ethical* than what morality allows for. Ethical attunement disrupts universalizing moral frameworks that would dictate how people deal with oppression. It enables exploration, collective questioning, and responsiveness that is tuned to the situation at hand.

In a widely circulated article entitled "Calling IN: A Less Disposable Way of Holding Each Other Accountable," Ngọc Loan Trần explains how calling out can feed into destructive ways of relating:

> Most of us know the drill. Someone says something that supports the oppression of another community, the red flags pop up and someone swoops in to call them out.
>
> But what happens when that someone is a person we know — and love? What happens when we ourselves are that someone?
>
> And what does it mean for our work to rely on how we have been programmed to punish people for their mistakes?

I'll be the first person and the last person to
say that anger is valid. Mistakes are mistakes; they
deepen the wounds we carry. I know that for me
when these mistakes are committed by people who I
am in community with, it hurts even more. But these
are people I care deeply about and want to see on the
other side of the hurt, pain, and trauma: I am willing
to offer compassion and patience as a way to build
the road we are taking but have never seen before.[27]

Whereas morality tends towards universal answers, certainties, and binary thinking, Trân recovers space for openness and uncertainty in the concept of "calling in," pointing
to the ways that people are supporting each other in naming
harm and violence and undoing it together. Trân goes on to
say that calling in is not about being soft or nice but instead
about tuning in to the complexities and relationships of
each situation when dealing with harm and mistakes:

I don't propose practicing "calling in" in opposition to calling out. I don't think that our work has
room for binary thinking and action. However, I
do think that it's possible to have multiple tools,
strategies, and methods existing simultaneously. It's
about being strategic, weighing the stakes and figuring out what we're trying to build and how we are
going to do it together.[28]

In this sense, calling in can be understood as a common
notion: not a fixed way of being or even a recommendation

but a practice that can be developed collectively, with transformative effects, and shared with caution. It is resonant with other common notions that have developed elsewhere, such as "leaning in" and "meeting people where they're at." It is an invitation to tune into the specificities and relationships in each situation rather than falling back on the prescriptions and justifications of morality.

Ethical attunement might include firm boundaries and aggressive call-outs. It might include attunement to one's own exhaustion, resulting in a refusal to engage at all. We find that ethical attunement thrives most as a *collective* process of experimentation. Like the concepts of infinite responsibility and emergent trust, it is sustained through a willingness to make mistakes and to allow others to make them, rather than trying to avoid being wrong. It's ultimately about the shared capacity to take care of each other in the face of pain, hurt, and violence.

There is always the risk of a concept like calling in being recaptured by liberal morality, adding a new set of norms to govern the conduct of people who are already dealing with systemic oppression: *be nice, take care of people, don't get so angry.* Therefore we want to be unequivocal, especially as white people, that we are *not* trying to establish new norms of conduct for conversations about oppression or to suggest that call-outs are wrong or counterproductive. Morality can prop up white fragility, white guilt, savior complexes, and other moves to innocence. It can enforce the idea that there is some duty to have these conversations over and over, extracting emotional labor from colonized people or people of color as if it were an

obligation. Liberal morality can hide the white suprema-
cist violence pervading schools, policing, and the prison
industrial complex, reducing racism to questions of individual guilt and inducing defensive reactions from white
people: *it's not my fault, I'm not racist, I haven't done anything wrong.*

Morality can sometimes *also* be behind tendencies *to
replace innocence with sin*, enabling white anti-racism that
creates barriers to undoing white supremacy. As we are
white people, moralism can induce us to loudly *proclaim*
our knowledge that we are racist, and to self-righteously call
out racism in others. Anti-racist organizer Chris Crass and
others have argued that there is a class dimension to this:

> For anti-racist work with a middle class orienta-
> tion, this then often looks like an over-emphasis on
> changing personal behavior, using correct language,
> and calling out other people who aren't acting and
> speaking in the right way. It can lead to a look-
> ing down on the communities that you have come
> from and distancing yourself from your own past
> by ruthlessly criticizing everyone who acts and talks
> like you did two weeks ago.[29]

Crass goes on to link these middle-class tendencies
to perfectionism and a fear of making mistakes. At the
same time, he makes it clear that this is not an attack on
the people reproducing these tendencies but on Empire's
forms of subjection:

> The enemy is capitalism, not middle class activists.
> And a middle class orientation isn't something that
> only middle class people can have, it's the orienta-
> tion that all of us who aren't ruling class are raised
> to endlessly and exhaustingly strive for.[30]

Feminism, disability justice, decolonization, Black
liberation, and other interconnected currents are short-cir-
cuiting individualizing moralism with much more complex
stories about oppression. Stories about institutionalized
white supremacy do not blame individual white people,
but they do not let us off the hook either: they reveal the
ways that we are participating in a system that stretches far
beyond us, *and* they compel us to discover ways to disrupt
that system by supporting anti-racist struggles. They attune
us to relationships and histories and deepen response-ability, not the the prescription of fixed duties, but by growing
capacities to be responsive to a whole range of collectively
formulated problems.

Common notions are emerging all the time against the
grain of moralism. These conversations are already happening in ways that get beyond dichotomies of rightness and
wrongness towards more complex *questions*. This can be
seen when people are able to draw out other ways of being
with each other, activating collective responses to violence.
It can be seen in disruptive tactics of direct action and in
the quiet forms of healing and being present with others. It
can be seen in the strategic use of privilege and in the ways
that people plant seeds and trust others to reach their own
conclusions.

Transformative responses like these are joyful in the Spinozan sense; they lead not to an increase in happiness but to an increase in one's capacity to affect and be affected, with all the pain and risk and uncertainty this might entail. Joy is never a duty and never something imposed on other people. We are not saying people *should* be ethically attuned. We are trying to affirm that joyful transformation is already happening, as an emergent power that undoes moralism and opens up new potentials, sometimes even beautifully. Joy subsists through common notions, which need to be held and tended in order to remain alive. As Ursula K. Le Guin writes in *The Lathe of Heaven*, "Love doesn't just sit there, like a stone. It has to be made, like bread; remade all the time, made new."[31]

You're so paranoid, you probably think this section is about you[32]

Lack-finding, perfectionism, schooling, walking

What follows is a third story about the origins of rigid radicalism, guided by these questions: What makes it possible, or even predictable, for radical spaces and movements to be perceived in terms of their shortcomings? What encourages the suspicion and incessant critique that runs through so many radical milieus? Is there something that makes critique a reflex and a habit and forces out other possibilities?

One example is learning to walk: when little kids take their first steps, people around them cheer, rejoice, and celebrate. We take photos, tell friends, and record these moments because we want to share the joy in witnessing the emergence of a new increase in capacity: *this kid is learning to walk!* But if we take a perfectionist perspective, then why celebrate? The kid won't usually walk for very long; they stumble and fall, and they certainly can't run. But no one says "Why are you celebrating? They're not *really* walking yet!"

If the kid learning to walk is just another kid walking, it's no longer something worth celebrating. Those who celebrate it are naïve or getting a bit carried away: kids are learning to walk all the time. But in the moment, it doesn't seem naïve, because we are part of the process of witnessing *this* kid walk, *in this way,* for the very first time.

We bring up this example because it seems obvious that it is nonsensical to impose external ideals of walking on little kids who are just learning, or to approach the situation with a detached and suspicious stance. It seems obvious (we hope) that a toddler's increase in capacity—those first steps that mark the emergence of something new—is sufficient in itself. It is a joyful moment, worth celebrating, not because it's part of some linear process of development but because it's an *emergent power* for that kid, palpable to all present in those moments.

With this in mind, why is it so difficult sometimes to celebrate small victories or humble increases in collective power and capacity? What makes it so easy to dismiss transformation as too limited? What makes it so easy to find joy lacking? We see variants of this dynamic happen a lot: someone celebrates something joyful, while others offer up reminders of its insufficiency. We find ourselves doing the same thing sometimes. What allows for the constant imposition of external norms, criteria, and ideals for evaluation?

Surely it comes from many different places, but we think part of it can be traced to the ways schooling crushes openness to new encounters. Most of us have been exposed to at least some of this for big chunks of our lives: schooling replaces curiosity with instruction, memorization, and hierarchical evaluation. We are encouraged to internalize the notion that our worth is connected to our grades, that we are locked in competition with our classmates, and that we are like empty vessels awaiting knowledge.

Not long after children learn to walk, they are often stuck in schools and subjected to constant monitoring, control, and evaluation. In school, new capacities can only be affirmed when they conform to the criteria set out by the institution; that is, when a student has learned a particular thing, at the right time, in the right way. Curiosity and the discovery of emergent connections need to be crushed in order to create this conformity, and those who refuse or resist are quickly labeled "problem" children, in need of remedial education, medication, therapy, or punishment.

Those who make it through learn to internalize incessant evaluation by externally imposed standards. By reducing lives to these external standards, schooling crushes the capacity for joy. Adults, parents, and other caregivers are tasked with continuing this process outside of school, teaching children to categorize and measure everything, including themselves. There is always someone further along, who has done it better and more proficiently. Evaluation works by removing the immediacy of life where we can sense the unfurling of newness and potential and learn by exploring the world, following our curiosities.

Radical perfectionism and paranoid reading

This tendency for constant evaluation and the imposition of external standards has percolated its way into many facets of life under Empire. It exists even among radicals: what changes is merely the kind of standards and the mode of evaluation. Is it radical? Is it anarchist? Is it critical? Is it revolutionary? Is it anti-oppressive? How might it be co-opted, complicit, or flawed? What is problematic? What does it fail to do? How limited, ineffective, and short-lived is it? Margaret Killjoy spoke to us about the ways that these tendencies can pervade anarchist spaces:

> While I think there's a decent bit of spontaneity and not-making-rules and such going on in radicalism, I see an awful lot less creativity at the moment. Particularly, I see very little creativity from tactical, strategic, and even theoretical analysis.... For a bunch of *anarchists*, we're remarkably uncomfortable with new ideas. If I were to hazard a guess, I would say that happens because we've really honed our ability to critique things but not our ability to embrace things.[33]

Applied incessantly, critique can become a reflex that forces out other capacities. The queer theorist Eve

Sedgwick argues that this penchant for constant critique runs through many currents of radical thought, in what she calls *paranoid reading*.[34] Paranoid reading is based on a stance of suspicion: an attempt to avoid co-optation or mistakes through constant vigilance. It seeks to ward off bad surprises by ensuring that oppression and violence are already known, or at least anticipated, so that one will not be caught off guard and so that one can react to the first sign of trouble. The result is that one is *always on guard and never surprised.* By approaching everything with detached suspicion, one closes off the capacity to be affected in new ways.

When we interviewed Richard Day, he suggested that this tendency is linked to being in pain and converting that pain into an incessant search for lack:

> In general, I think rigid radicalism is a response to feeling really hurt and fucked up. And the real enemy is the dominant order, but it gets mixed into this big soup, so the enemy becomes each other. It becomes oneself. It's a finding lacking as such ... a finding lacking almost everywhere with almost everyone. And when that lack is found, then of course there needs to be some action: which is going to be to tell, or force, or coerce, or get at that lack, and try to turn it into a wholeness. So, strangely enough, I'd suggest that rigid radicalism is driven by a desire to heal. And it has exactly the opposite effect: of sundering the self more, of sundering communities more, and so on.[35]

Those of us who regularly find ourselves in pain might find this paradox familiar. Through the constant imposition of external standards, everything can be found lacking, and all kinds of coercive responses can seem justified. An endless cycle ensues: no one and nothing is good enough, and this paranoid stance constantly incapacitates exploration, healing, and affirmation.

Many of us learn this mode of thought through university or through immersion in radical spaces themselves: we learn to search for, anticipate, and point out the pervasiveness of Empire. Even without the sad rigor of the Weather Underground, we learn to search the bodies, behaviors, and words of others for any shred of complicity. Mik Turje spoke to this tendency:

> I think as a youth I was really idealistic, and I came to the university context, and critical theory, where idealism and imagining something better was stamped out as something naïve. The only option was to master the hypercritical language myself, and one-upping people. I got really good at that. I won all of the political arguments in school, but ... I was being a shitbag of a militant, tearing everyone down.[36]

By being immersed in paranoid reading, people learn to find themselves and others lacking. Having been "educated," one becomes a pedagogue oneself, spreading the word about Empire, oppression, and violence, and in the process one tends to position others as naïve and ignorant.

This is clear in how surprise and curiosity are often *infantilized* by Empire. They are treated as foolish or "childish"—that is, lacking the *educated, rational, civilized, adult* capacities of detached evaluation. Paranoid reading and its association with adulthood and rational detachment are transmitted through schooling, founded on patriarchal white supremacy. Based on suspicion, perfectionism, and the penchant for finding flaws in ourselves and others, paranoid reading prevents us from being joyfully in touch with the world and with the always already present potential for transformation.

Crucially, paranoid reading and lack-finding have their own affective ecology, with their own pleasures and rewards. There can be a sense of satisfaction in being the one who anticipates or exposes inadequacy. There can be safety and comfort in a paranoid stance, because it helps ensure that we already know what to do with new encounters. Incessantly exposing flaws can be pleasurable and can even become a source of belonging.

We think this is at the heart of what destroys the transformative potential of movements from within: the capacity for paranoid reading closes off the capacity to embrace and be embraced by new things. The stance of detached judgment means remaining at a distance from what is taking place. In contrast, experimentation requires openness and vulnerability, including the risk of being caught off guard or hurt. From a paranoid perspective, things like gratitude, celebration, curiosity, and openness are naïve at best and potentially dangerous. When everything is anticipated or one can see immediately how something is imperfect or lacking, one misses the capacity to be affected and *moved*.

Holding ambivalence

Beyond mere happiness, what is being crushed by paranoid reading and lack-finding is all the ambivalence and messy intensity of transformation. Walidah Imarisha evokes this powerfully in her book, *Angels with Dirty Faces*, in which she shares the moment when she and other prison abolition organizers learned that Haramia, one of their imprisoned comrades, has had his death sentence commuted after a long struggle:

> "The governor commuted his sentence!" Haramia's campaign organizer smiled brighter than the sun beating down on us.
>
> "It's the first time Perry ever did it! The Board of Pardons voted 6-1 for clemency—they haven't voted to stop an execution in 25 years. We did it! We won!"
>
> Silence. Incredulousness. Too scared to believe, to hope.
>
> Then the explosion—yelling, hugging, crying ....
>
> They commuted Haramia's sentence to life in prison. On an LA radio interview, I spoke of this victory. A woman called in: "But he's still in prison, for life. Isn't that a death sentence too? How can you call this a win?"
>
> I paused. "We won a battle in the larger war. We know that tomorrow we have to get up to continue. Tonight we celebrate. We celebrate that tomorrow,

Haramia will see another dawn. Today ... today was
a good day."

We took over the prison yard, the supporters.
Sprawled out on the grass. Screamed the good news
into cell phones. Fell into each other's arms, laugh-
ing. Unable to give words to my feelings, I somer-
saulted across the prison lawn. It was the first time
I ever felt truly joyous in a prison yard, without a
sense of dread and sadness nestled underneath.

It was the only time I saw guards do absolutely
nothing as we broke every prison conduct rule,
written and unwritten. They knew we won that day.

I couldn't help but feel Hasan's presence.[37]
Smiling his child-like grin. Whispering softly,
"Yeah, Wa Wa, enjoy it now.

"Tomorrow we got a lot more work to do."[38]

Imarisha's story evokes the intensity of this moment,
palpable even to the prison guards: it was enough to disrupt, if only for a few moments, the brutal and arbitrary
rules of the prison. The event punched a hole in the ultra-
controlled space of the prison.

Imarisha makes clear the importance of celebration,
even as the ambivalence of the victory was obvious. Only
from a perspective of comparative evaluation and paranoid reading is it possible to remind oneself and others that
the key point to focus on is that Haramia is still in prison
or that the prison industrial complex is still intact. Only
when viewed from a distance, without the investments and
connections of those involved, could one think that this

celebration is naïve or unfounded. Imarisha spoke to this when we interviewed her:

> In a society that fits everything into dichotomy, you win or you lose. There is no space for a win that is attached to a loss. In the case of Haramia KiNassor, whose death sentence was commuted, it was an immense win to have that brotha still with us. And other people were executed that same week by the state of Texas. And his comrade Hasan Shakur who was also my close compañer@ was executed almost a year before to the day. So for me the win and loss of the situation was ever present, breathing together. And it's really hard to hold both of those.[39]

Imarisha's words reveal the capacity to hold on to intensity and ambivalence, without parsing it into a binary between "feeling good" and "feeling bad," or setting optimism against pessimism. To be capable of holding all of this—of wins attached to losses and joys attached to sorrows—is fundamentally about being *affected*. It is about inhabiting a world of uncertainty and complexity, about feeling and participating in emergent and collective powers. Joy.

What all of this makes clear to us is that there is no formula for a break with paranoid reading: there is only the discovery and renewal of ways of moving and relating, right where we are, in our own lives. To undo paranoid reading entails more than "being nice" or "not alienating people." It can be about openness to new encounters and putting relationships before ideas. It requires challenging the corrosive tendency that impels us to find lack everywhere, to outmeasure, to out-preach, and to be on guard against mistakes and the unexpected. It entails recovering the capacities to celebrate and to be surprised.

The limits of critique: from paranoia to potential

Radical and incisive critique is an indispensable weapon. In a world where we are enmeshed in forms of subjection, critique can support resistance and transformation. It can be a source of intimate reflection, unpacking things that are already sensed intuitively. By revealing that things have not always been this way, and that they could be different, critique can create wiggle-room for struggle. At the same time, when reduced to a habit, a reflex, or an end in itself, critique can become stifling and paranoid. And, we must admit, pointing to paranoid reading and perfectionism can itself become a new form of paranoia: a critique of critique.

These are the limits of critique. Critique can be helpful for asking how subtle dynamics manifest themselves or for questioning inherited ways of doing things, but it doesn't necessarily activate capacities to be different with each other.

For this reason, we want to emphasize the potential of affirmative theory as a complementary *power* that might help ward off paranoia. We talked to Silvia Federici about this because we have been struck by the way she combines an incisive critique of Empire with an incredible generosity towards movements. Her approach is not about being positive all the time but about the *potential* of struggle:

CARLA AND NICK: Another thing that we wanted to talk to you about is the style and tone of intellectual engagement. You have a really militant critique of capitalism, but you're always pointing to inspiring examples in a range of different movements, and you seem to reserve critique, in terms of a really pointed attack, for large destructive institutions like the World Bank. So we wanted to ask: is this style something that you've cultivated and that you're intentional about? And maybe more generally, can you talk about the potential of theory in intellectual work today? What makes theory enabling and transformative, and what gets in the way of that?

FEDERICI: It's partially a consequence of growing old. You understand things that when you're younger you didn't see. One thing that I've learned is to be more humble and hold my judgment of people until I know them beyond what I can make out from what they say, realizing that people often say foolish things that they do not really believe or have not seriously thought about.

It also comes from recognizing that we can change, which means that we should stress our potential rather than our limits. One of the most amazing experiences in the women's movement was to see how much we could grow, learning to speak in public, write poetry, make beautiful posters. All this has given me a strong distaste for the impulse to squash everything at the first sign that something is not right.

I've made it a principle not to indulge in speech that is destructive. Striving to speak clearly, not to make people feel like fools because they don't understand what I say, is a good part of it. That's also something I've taken from the women's movement. So many times we had felt humiliated, being in situations where we didn't understand what men had said and didn't have the courage to ask what they meant. I don't want to make other people ever feel this way.[40]

The notion of stressing potential, rather than limits seems very important to us. This is not just a shift in focus but a whole different orientation. Limits are often spoken of as if they are fixed, and paranoid reading specializes in locating them and pointing them out. But limits are never fixed. Limits are the always shifting edges of what we are, what we are capable of. To explore potential is to live right at these fluid edges. Affirmative reading is rooted in Spinoza's insight that we do not know in advance what a body—or a movement or struggle—can *do*. This ignorance is what makes experimentation possible. *Potential* is the dimension of these unfolding encounters that can never be known beforehand.

To replace paranoid reading with affirmation is about activating a power complementary to critique, without giving up on critical thinking. Reading affirmatively and seeking out potentials can be a way for us to find new resonances and experiment with concepts in new ways. Critique—as the questioning of inherited certainties and habits—might be necessary to remove the obstacles to all this exploration. It might tear apart some of the rigidities that make experimentation difficult. But it can fall into a paranoid search for problems, detached from the immediacy of life and the potential of new encounters. Maybe some paranoia is necessary—just because you're paranoid doesn't mean they aren't out to get you. Maybe it is a question of dosage and mixture, timing and framing, of combining critique and curiosity, wariness and exploration. We are not sure.

Towards new encounters

Wherever they appear, common notions and transformative movements can fall prey to rigid radicalism. The shift can be subtle: what worked in a particular place and time can be converted into a fixed how-to list. A sense of experimentation and vitality can be sucked out of the air with a few words that induce a sense of paranoia and lack-finding. The shared capacity for encounters across difference can be converted into moral certainty and guilt-mongering. What was initially transformative in one context can be held up as *the* answer, a new duty, or a new set of responsibilities that are imposed on others. This can even manifest as a rigid insistence on autonomy and individual freedom that crushes the potential for collective responsibility and action.

Ethics and uncertainty cannot survive long in an atmosphere of stagnation and rigidity. Detached from the transformative relationships that animate them, common notions become fixed principles dropped on other people's heads. They remain enabling and ethical only insofar as they retain the capacity to activate response-ability: the capacity to ask, over and over again, what might move things here and now, and to really take pause and listen to each other deeply. All of this is to say that ethical attunement, experimentation, and common notions are powerful, fragile, and precious. These sensibilities are already emerging in a lot of places, as people figure out how to sustain and defend joy against the crushing tendencies of both Empire and rigid radicalism.

Paranoid reading, moralism, and ideology aren't going anywhere, and even naming and criticizing them can be ways of slipping into their poisonous grip, giving one a sense of superiority, of being *above* all those things. The critique of rigid radicalism can manifest as a new way of finding mistakes or as contempt for places and people (including oneself) where rigid radicalism takes hold. It can become a paranoid critique of paranoia itself: criticism might be helpful to get a little distance from stifling and hurtful dynamics or in figuring out how they work, but it will not necessarily activate other ways of being. Critiques are no use unless they create openings for joy and experimentation and for feeling and acting differently. For us, the best way to do this analytically has been to affirm that openings are already happening and always have been and that it is worth being grateful for these powerful legacies.

In our own experience and in talking with others, becoming otherwise is never a linear passage from one way of being to another but instead a slow, uneven, messy process. Sometimes something new emerges only in the wreckage after groups have torn each other apart, or have people "burned out." Sometimes the flight from paranoid reading flips over into an everything-is-awesome attitude that refuses all forms of discernment and critique. Sometimes people sense that things are not working, find bits of joy, but then rigid radicalism takes over again in another guise. Sometimes a dramatic event leads to new common notions and joyful ways of relating, and rigid radicalism loses its grip. Sometimes people abandon rigid radicalism in favor of an attempt to live a "normal" life under Empire. Sometimes people travel, and their encounters leave them changed, more capable of cultivating collective power and experimentation. There is no blueprint, no map for moving in other ways.

In telling these stories, we have tried to avoid generating prescriptions for others, and we hope to have made space for a proliferation of other stories about rigid radicalism, especially those about how and where people have been able to undo it or relate differently. New potentials can be activated by continuing these conversations with each other.

Ultimately, we think, what is at stake in undoing rigid radicalism is joyful transformation: a proliferation of forms of life that cannot be governed by Empire or stifled by rigid radicalism. To be militant about this is to nurture and defend these shared powers that grow through people's capacities to tune in to their own situations, to remain open and experimental, and to recover and invent enabling forms of combat and intimacy.

Outro

This is a book that does not have an ending. It is a definition that negates itself in the same breath. It is a question, an invitation to discuss.[1]

—John Holloway

It can be difficult to talk about the ways that radical milieus can be stifling and rigid: how we don't always treat each other well, how we hurt each other, and how shame, rigidity, and competition can creep into the very movements and spaces that are trying to undo all this. Of course there are tangles of despair, resentment, pleasure, and pain. Of course shitty encounters provoke anxieties and frustrations. Of course people bring their scars and fears. In his interview, Glen Coulthard put his finger on something we have carried with us throughout this process, about the way that sadness and anger often stem from love:

> I think that for the somber, melancholic militant, I get it. I understand it. How could you not be?

And this is my point—the only way you respond to
the world like that is because of some base sort of
individual and collective self-respect. Some love for
oneself and others, or the land, that you see being
violated in a profound way. This produces melan-
choly, anger, whatever. They're not separable. So
when we're leveling our critiques, you just have to
understand that, yeah, it's a rational response to an
irrational, violent, unthinking machinery. So how
do we direct that in ways that are able to topple
these power relationships? And that's when the
kind of navel-gazing, defensive, puritanical radical
becomes an obstacle, even though they may right-
fully be that way, because of the position that they
occupy. And the process of redirection comes from
community, a community that we aspire towards
and is always already there. So that's the question:
What do we do with that situation? How do we
make that community stronger? I don't know what
the answer is, but the question is there, or else we
wouldn't be having this conversation. We need it to
be there more, with more people.[2]

We have attempted to approach rigid radicalism with
care, so that we wouldn't just be finding movements lacking in a whole new way. We have tried to convey a conversation, a set of questions rather than a set of answers. How
do we talk about rigid radicalism in a way that doesn't just
heap more shit at the feet of those who are already fighting?
What can support conversations that provide space to think

and feel through all this in milieus and movements? How can we pull each other into other ways of being together?

We have suggested that rigid radicalism is not a solid thing outside of us but an affective tendency we are amid. It circulates, constricts, suffocates, recirculates. It brings its own pleasures and rewards. Maybe it is driven in part by a desire to heal.

The real enemy is Empire itself, and rigid radicalism is a poisonous reaction that presents itself as the cure. As such, rigid radicalism is one of the ways that Empire calls forth some desires and attachments and conjures away others, keeping its subjects stuck in a desolate form of life. In the twilight of Empire's legitimacy, it has become more and more difficult to sustain the fantasy that capitalism is good for us or that elected leaders represent us. Governments announce sustainability initiatives alongside new forms of resource extraction, multiculturalism alongside militarized policing. But Empire doesn't need our faith, only our compliance. As Empire's subjects, we are increasingly fastened to an automated, industrialized infrastructure that consumes and poisons the living world. Through the glow of our screens, we are induced to express ourselves in perpetual performance and collective surveillance. The crisis is not coming: it is already here. It has been here for a long time, and Empire is administering the wreckage. We are permitted to be as cynical and pessimistic as we want, as long as we remain detached from capacities to live and relate differently.

In this sense, Empire cannot be confronted only by inculcating others with the right set of anticapitalist and antistate beliefs. People do not need some special training or education to be capable of transformation. On the contrary, we are constantly trained *away* from aliveness to change. It is not a question of being right but of assembling enabling ways of thinking, doing, and feeling in the present. This is most palpable in exceptional situations of disaster and insurrection, when everyday people have a little space from Empire's exhausting anxieties and routines. Amid a lot of suffering and scarcity, there are upwellings of mutual aid and connection. This is not evidence of some innate altruism. For us, it is evidence that everyone is capable of joyful transformation, and the ongoing disaster is the brutal isolation and exploitation of life organized by Empire. An increase in the capacity to affect and be affected—joy—means being more in touch with a world that is bleeding, burning, screaming.

Transformation might begin with rage, hatred, or sorrow. Refusing to "get over" some things can cut against the grain of obligatory productivity and optimism structuring capitalist life. Shared power might arise from accepting, refusing, hanging on, or letting go. This is the wiggle room of freedom: not the absence of constraint or a do-what-you-like individualism but an emergent capacity to work on relationships, shift desires, and undo ingrained habits.

We believe that close ties of friendship and kinship, far from isolating us into cliques or enclaves, actually enable people to better extend themselves to others and participate in transformative encounters. Close friends and loved ones are what enable us to gripe and vent so that we can be more compassionate and patient with those who don't know us as well. They help us process fears and anxieties so that we are better able to trust people up front and move towards trouble and discomfort. They sit with us when we inevitably fuck up and flail. In turn, transformative struggle can deepen these bonds and generate new ones.

We have suggested that the challenge is not to build a unified consciousness or position but to find ways of coming together, collaborating, fighting, and discovering shared affinities. This is not about everyone getting along and becoming friends. Vulnerability is important but also risky and needs to be selective. As Coulthard said, "Some relationships are just bullshit, and we shouldn't be in them. We should actually draw lines in the sand more willingly." Joy needs sharp edges to thrive. How to create spaces, then, where vulnerability can happen and joyful encounters can take place? When to be open, and to what, and how to create and maintain boundaries? What can we do together? How can we support each other? How to create space for consensus *and* dissensus and difference? How to ward off imperatives to centralize and control things without creating new divisions and sectarian conflicts? How to ward off rigid radicalism and its attachments to purity and paranoia?

These are all ethical questions that people are exploring rather than answering once and for all. We have suggested that in the space between abstract morality and vapid individualism, common notions can help us remain open and responsive.

In a world of crushing monopolies, where so much is done to us or for us, some people are recovering the capacity to do things for themselves. From barricades to kitchen tables, they are generating collective forms of trust and responsibility. If such forms make people feel alive, if they deepen bonds of trust and love, militancy tends to grow along with them because people are willing to defend these emergent powers. Every moment that people find trust in each other and in their own capacities is precious. Through these messy struggles, people are becoming powerful and dangerous together.

To be *militant about joy* means forging common notions that can enable, sustain, and deepen transformation here and now, starting from wherever people find themselves. Common notions are not a means to a revolution in the future but the recovery of people's capacities for autonomy and struggle here and now. This tends towards breaking down old divides between organizing and everyday existence, and opening the question of collective life itself in all its expansiveness. Nurturing common notions means refusing to separate the effectiveness of any tactic or strategy from its *affectiveness*: how it makes people feel, how it nurtures autonomy or dependence, what it opens up, and what it closes down.[3] It means letting go of practices or ideas when they stagnate, and generating new ones together. Rather than fixed values or positions, in common notions we find ways of doing, thinking, and feeling that sustain the growth of shared power.

With the concept of joyful militancy, we have tried to affirm these other ways of being without pretending that we have discovered the answer to undoing Empire, warding off rigid radicalism, or ushering in some world revolution. There is no single answer. We have tried to avoid setting up joyful militancy as a new ideal to embody or a set of duties.

It would be disappointing if the notion of joyful militancy ever became a handbook for transformation because it lives in questions, experiments, and openings—not answers, blueprints, or necessities.

Three modes of attunement

We think people's militancy and autonomy—their capacity to grapple with oppression, to break from comfort and certainty in favor of risk, to maintain forms of life that do not reproduce the state and capitalism—depend on participation in transformative struggles. With this in mind, we are interested in capacities to tune into transformative potential.

One mode of attunement involves increasing sensitivity and inhabiting situations more fully. It is in this sense that Amador Fernandez-Savater suggests that the revolutionary alternative to control consists in "learning to fully inhabit, instead of governing, a process of change. Letting yourself be affected by reality, to be able to affect it in turn. Taking time to grasp the possibles that open up in this or that moment." What if the capacity to be really present is revolutionary? What potentials can be unleashed by connecting with the immediate, in a world that encourages constant distraction, deferral, and numbness?

Crucially, this attunement is not a new form of optimism or a newfound faith that things will get better but something open-ended and dangerous. This capacity to be present, what adrienne maree brown called "being awake inside your life in real time," includes more of the messy multiplicities that we are: trauma, triggers, *and* brilliance. Joy is not the same as optimism. It is not happy, nor does it promise a future revolution. In fact, being present might be a way of tuning into the cruelty and self-destruction of certain optimistic attachments.[4]

A second form of attunement comes through the capacity to connect with legacies of resistance, rebellion, and the struggles of the past. As Silvia Federici explained when we interviewed her, this is a pushing-back against the social amnesia imposed by Empire:

> What most matters is discovering and re-creating the collective memory of past struggles. In the US there is a systematic attempt to destroy this memory, and now this is extending across the world, with the destruction of the main historical centers of the Middle East—a form of dispossession that has major consequences and yet is rarely discussed. Reviving the memory of the struggles of the past makes us feel part of something larger than our individual lives, and in this way it gives a new meaning to what we are doing and gives us courage because it makes us less afraid of what can happen to us individually.[5]

Reviving legacies of struggle can be a source of dignity and inspiration amid forces that seem implacable. In this sense, transformation is not about the modern vision of shucking off traditions and escaping the past. History can also help us tune into the *ongoingness* of antagonisms that

Empire has attempted to relegate to the past. It can help us see and feel the ways that Empire's institutions have been resisted since their inception.

As cis-gendered white folks, we have a lot to learn from Black folks, Indigenous people, people of color, and queer and trans folks who have long resisted Empire's violence while nurturing alternatives. There is also a lot to be learned from others whose knowledge and capacities continue to be devalued and whose existence entails resistance; for us that often means looking to the kids in our lives and community for guidance and inspiration. We have suggested that we all have the capacity to recover our own traditions and engage in our own struggles (rather than appropriating others') and to explore affinities between them in ways that challenge and undo the interconnected violence of Empire.

A final mode of attunement to potential is gratitude and celebration. Especially among white, secular radicals, gratitude is often seen as a "hippie" value: something associated with New Age gurus and self-help manuals that insist that positive thinking can overcome any obstacle. Gratitude and celebration are often seen as superfluous or even counterproductive, as if feeling grateful requires turning away from the horrors of Empire or losing the desire for change. But as Walidah Imarisha suggested, celebration or gratitude can mean holding wins attached to losses and letting them breathe together. Grief can be attached to gratitude, pleasure to pain, and celebration to determination. Similarly, Zainab Amadahy emphasizes the power of gratitude to renew our connection to the forces that sustain life, among human and nonhuman relationships:

You can be thankful and still want the world to be better; want your life to be better. At the same time, I don't think it's healthy to be grateful in every moment. Sometimes grief, sadness, or fear is the appropriate and healthy response. But when the crisis has passed or it's a chronic situation, focusing one's attention on what there is to be grateful for literally eases the pain—physical, mental, and emotional.[6]

Throughout this project we have tried to center relationships in a process of walking with questions. The book has morphed and changed in significant ways as we listened and were challenged by friends and each other. Leaving space for emergence and uncertainty was frustrating, inspiring, difficult, and ultimately generative of a messy, joyful process.

With this in mind, we want to share our gratitude to all those who are resisting and undoing Empire starting from their own situations. Thank you to those who are leaning into the uncertain work of transformation. Thank you to those who are fiercely defending the people and places they love. Thank you to those who are keeping their own traditions and forms of life alive and dangerous amid forces seeking to annihilate and absorb them.

Thank you to everyone who is part of this book. Thank you to those we interviewed, who encouraged us and challenged us to think in new ways. Thank you to everyone who has been part of this conversation informally and supported us and offered insights and care. Thank you to our readers for your curiosity, your critical engagement, and your capacity to cultivate joy.

Appendix 1: Feeling Powers Growing—An Interview with Silvia Federici

January 18, 2016

SILVIA FEDERICI: My politics resonate with your idea of "joyful militancy." I'm a strong believer that either your politics is liberating and that gives you joy, or there's something wrong with them.

I've gone through phases of "sad politics" myself, and I've learned to identify the mistakes that generate it. It has many sources. But one factor is the tendency to exaggerate the importance of what we can do by ourselves, so that we always feel guilty for not accomplishing enough.

When I was thinking about this conversation, I was reminded of Nietzsche's metamorphoses in *Thus Spoke Zarathustra* and his image of the camel. The camel is the prototype of the militant who burdens herself with huge amounts of work, because she thinks that the destiny of the world depends on her overwork. Inevitably she's always saddened because the goal is always receding and she does not have the time to be fully present to her life and recognize the transformative possibilities inherent to her work.

NICK AND CARLA: You said that you feel like there are so many sources to sad militancy, and can you speak to some more of those?[1]

FEDERICI: Sad militancy comes from setting goals that you cannot achieve, so that the outcome is always out of reach, always projected into the future, and you feel continuously defeated. "Sad politics " is also defining your struggle in purely oppositional terms, which puts you in a state of permanent tension and failure. A joyful politics is a politics that is constructive and prefigurative. I'm encouraged by the fact that more people today see that you cannot continuously postpone the achievement of your goals to an always receding future.

Joyful politics is politics that change your life for the better already in the present. This is not to deny that political engagement often involves suffering. In fact our political involvement often is born of suffering. But the joy is knowing and deciding that we can do something about it; it is recognizing that we share our pain with other people, is feeling the solidarity of those around us. Militants in Argentina speak of "politicizing our sadness."

This is why I don't believe in the concept of "self-sacrifice," where self-sacrifice means that we do things that go against our needs, our desires, our potentials, and for the sake of political work we have to repress ourselves. This has been a common practice in political movements in the past. But it is one that produces constantly dissatisfied individuals. Again, what we do may lead to suffering, but this may be preferable to the kind of self-destruction we would have faced had we remained inactive.

The inability to make politics a rewarding experience is part of the reason why, I think, the radical Left has been unsuccessful in attracting large numbers of people. Here too we are beginning to learn, however. I see that many young militants today are recognizing the importance of building community, of organizing activities that are pleasurable, that build trust and affective relations, like eating together, for instance. It is not an accident that Indigenous peoples' movements in Latin America give so much importance to the organization of events like the fiestas.

Nick and carla: We wanted to ask you specifically about the feminist movement and what are some of the ways that feminists and other movements have struggled with sad militancy in the past. We're thinking of Jo Freeman's essay on "trashing" from the '70s, where she talks about real tendencies to destroy relationships within the feminist movement.[2] In one of the interviews that you've done, you mention "truculent forms of behavior that were typical of the movement in the '60s" and that you see new forms of kindness and care emerging that maybe were absent back then. So we wanted to ask you about how things have changed from your perspective and whether you see a connection between trashing and what is now called call-out culture in contemporary movements.

FEDERICI: When I wrote about truculent behavior, I was thinking of relations in the male Left and male-dominated organizations, where you found a lot of protagonism and peacock-like competition, as well as a manipulation of women, sexual and otherwise. These were among the factors that motivated the rise of the women's liberation movement. Not only women's demands were pushed off the agenda, but everyday relations were often degrading for them.

A good description of women's lives in male-dominated organizations is Marge Piercy's *The Grand Coolie Dam*, where she powerfully describes the many forms of subordination women suffered in male-dominated groups.[3] In comparison, the organizational forms the women's movement adopted were a major improvement. Possibly feminists moved too far in the opposite direction. I am thinking of Jo Freeman's critique of the "tyranny of structurelessness."[4] But she's excessively critical of the feminist movement. I don't agree that feminists were especially prone to trashing each other. The attack on leadership, for instance, though it often worked against people's capacity to express themselves, also opened the way to more egalitarian relations—like ensuring that everyone would have a change to speak in a meeting. The resistence against women getting credit for authoring articles or speaking too much in public was a legacy of the experiences we had made in male-dominated organizations. In time, it is a fear that most women left behind, as they felt more confident in their own powers.

Some of the bitterness that you find in Jo Freeman comes perhaps from the fact that, when we joined the women's movement, many of us believed that we had reached a sort of paradise. As I wrote in "Putting Feminism on Its Feet," when I began to work with other women I truly felt that I had found my home, my tribe.[5] We thought that we had reached a place where everything would be harmonious; where there would be love, care, reciprocity, equality, cooperation—sisterhood as we called it. So we disactivated our critical thinking and left our defenses down. Unfortunately, we didn't reach paradise, and the disappointment was especially severe because we assumed that in the women's movement we would find happiness, or at least we would not encounter the kind of jealousies, power plays, and power relations we had experienced with men.

Spinoza speaks of joy as coming from reason and understanding. But we forgot that all of us bear on our bodies and minds the marks of life in a capitalist society. We forgot that we came to the feminist movement with many scars and fears. We would feel devalued and easily take offense if we thought we were not properly valued. It was a jealousy that came from poverty, from fear of not being given our due. This also led some women to be possessive about what they had done, what they had written or said.

These are all the classical problems and distortions that life in a capitalist society creates. Over time you learn to identify them, but at first many of us were devastated by them. For me, coping with this realization has been an important learning process. But I have also seen women leaving the movement because they were so deeply hurt by it.

On the other hand, the feminist movement, because it stressed the importance of sharing experiences and engaging in a collective examination of our everyday lives and problems, gave us important tools to deal with this situation. Through "consciousness-raising" and the refusal to separate politics from our everyday reproduction it created forms of organization that built trust and showed that our strength was rooted in our mutual solidarity.

I found a vision in the women's movement that allowed me to overcome some bitter experiences and over time insulated me from disappointment. I see politics now as a process of transformation, a process by which we learn to better ourselves, shed our possessiveness, and discard the petty squabbles that so much poison our lives.

I think that this has been a collective experience that has left a mark on other organizations as well. It seems to me that, over the last two or three decades, the women's movement has been the most important influence on the organizational forms of most radical movements. You don't find today, on a general level, the kind of behavior that was common among men thirty or forty years ago, not at least among the new generations, although there is still a good amount of machismo around. But you also have men who genuinely want to be feminist and define themselves as anti-patriarchal or organize against male supremacy—all unthinkable stands—with few exceptions—in the '60s.

CARLA: I have all these questions! There seems to be some kind of paradox in this: that joy is about feelings and relationships but not just an individual feeling. And while we want to speak to the power of joy, it can't be turned into a commandment, and in fact it gets lost when it becomes something imposed on people. But it also can't be about just feeling happy or feeling good or being okay with the way things are. It feels like a little bit of a paradox, and I haven't figured out how to think that through. A lot of my activism over the years has been around youth liberation and working with children having more of a say, and getting that form of oppression into the discussion and into activist spaces, and my work was very centered around that in a public way. I don't want to replicate individualism in liberation; I want it to always be connected to the larger systems and social struggles. But it also needs to be about thriving right now, because they're kids! And when things were working well it seemed that there was a lot of room for freedom and growth, but it was held and felt collectively, without a bunch of rules or norms. There was happiness, sure, but also difficulty and a willingness to work through it. So it feels like a constant paradox to work through joy....

FEDERICI: I like the distinction between happiness and joy. Like you, I like joy because it is an active passion. It's not a static state of being. And it's not satisfaction with things as they are. It's part of feeling powers and capacities growing within yourself and in the people around you. It's a feeling, a passion, that comes from a process of transformation and growth. It does not mean that you're satisfied with your situation. It means, again using Spinoza, that you're active in accordance to what your understanding tells you to do and what is required by the situation. So you feel that you have the power to change and feel yourself changing through what you're doing, together with other people. It's not a form of acquiescence to what exists.

NICK AND CARLA: We've found your concept of the accumulation of divisions really compelling, and the ways you're centering

how capitalism is always using white supremacy, patriarchy, colonization, and other oppressive hierarchies to create
divisions and enable exploitation. Your historicization of
those divisions is powerful because you show how the state
and capitalism have deepened and entrenched patriarchy
and racism as a strategy to stop resistance and enable more
intense exploitation. And for us, in this book we really want
to center the importance of rebuilding trust and connection
and solidarity across those divisions, while leaving space for
difference and autonomy. One of the things that we like
about your work is that you don't jump to a simple unity—
that overcoming these divisions doesn't look like a simple
unity. And so we wanted to ask you to talk about that a little more. Is there a distinction between divisions, which are
hierarchical and exploitative, and differences, which might
be something else? And can you talk about the positive
horizon you see for resisting the accumulation of divisions
while warding off a kind of homogenizing unity?

Federici: Yes, the distinction between differences and divisions
is important. When I speak of "divisions" I speak of differences that carry hierarchies, inequalities, and have a divisive
power. So we need to be very clear when we speak of "differences." Not all should be celebrated.

The lesson we learned in the '60s from the women's
movement and the Black Power movement is that the most
effective way to respond to unequal relations is for those
who have less social power to organize autonomously. This
does not exclude the possibility of coming together for particular struggles. But in a society divided along racial and
gender lines, unity is a goal to be achieved, not something

that can be assumed to already exist. Organizational autonomy, or at least the construction of autonomous spaces within mixed organizations—as it often happens in Latin America—is a necessary condition to subvert these divisions. The women's movement could not have developed the understanding of the situation of women that it developed if women had remained in male-dominated organizations. It was crucial for women to move away from these organizations to even begin to think about their problems and share their thoughts with each other.

You cannot think of a problem, give voice to it, share it with others, if you fear that you will be dismissed, ridiculed, or told that it is not important. Moreover, how could women have spoken of sexuality and their relations with men in front of them? And how could Black militants speak openly of their experience of racism in front of white people?

Autonomy within movements that are working towards unity but are traversed by power relations is fundamental. A crucial reality would have remained hidden if the feminist movement had not organized autonomously, and this is also true of the Black Power movement. Important areas and forms of exploitation would have continued to be unnoticed, would not have been analyzed and denounced, and would have continued to be reproduced.

NICK AND CARLA: You often point to Latin America and other places where the social fabric is much stronger in general, and movements are a lot more capable of reproducing themselves and meeting their own needs, relying less on the state and capital. The maintenance of communal and cooperative forms of life seems to be central to the capacity for sustained struggle and resistance. Can you elaborate on all this?

FEDERICI: I went to Nigeria in the '80s and one of the big surprises for me was to discover that large amounts of land were still managed communally. That doesn't mean that in communal land regimes relationships are necessarily egalitarian. Generally men have more power than women, but until recently they could not sell the land. Clearly these communal regimes have gone through many changes, especially because of colonial domination. But the fact that communal ownership has been widespread in Africa until at least the nineteenth century, and in some regions continues even today, has had a deep impact on relationships and people, which is why I believe so much violence has been and is necessary to privatize the land and the continent's immense natural resources.

It's the same thing in Latin America. In Mexico, in the 1930s, during the government of Lázaro Cárdenas, some land was returned to Indigenous communities that had been expropriated by colonial invasion. Today the Mexican government is trying to re-privatize everything, but until recently at least 30 percent of the country's land was still held communally.

Again, this is not a guarantee of egalitarian relations. Women in these communities are coming forward, criticizing the patriarchal relations often prevailing within them. A good example are the Zapatista women. As you can read in Hilary Klein's book *Compañeras*, many of the transformations that have taken place in Zapatista communities, like the application of the Revolutionary Law on Women, have been the product of the struggle that women have made against patriarchalism. But communal land regimes guarantee the reproduction of the communities that live on the land.

Today many of these communities are facing dispossession because of land privatization, deforestation, the loss of water to irrigate their milpas. But when they are forced out and come to the cities, they still act as a collectivity. They take over land though collective action, they build encampments and take decision collectively. As a result, in many cities of Latin America, new communities have formed that from their beginning were built collectively. It appears that the narcos now try to infiltrate some of these communities. But when people take over the land and cooperate to build their houses, to build the streets, to fight with the government to connect the electricity and get water pipes, there is a good chance that that they will be able to respond to this threat, and you can see that there's a new social reality emerging in these communities.

As Raúl Zibechi often points out, something new is emerging in these communities because they have had to invent new forms of life, without any preexisting model, and politicize the everyday process of their reproduction.[6] When you work together, building houses, building streets, building structures that provide some immediate form of health care—just to give some examples—you are making life choices, as all of them come with a high cost. You must fight the state, fight the police, the local authorities. So you have to develop tight relations with each other and always measure the value of all things.

NICK AND CARLA: Following up on that, part of what we are curious about is how we can learn from places where, in general, the degree of politicization is higher and the social fabric is much stronger. What kind of lessons can North American–based organizers draw from this for organizing in our own communities? How can people in the global North learn from all of the vibrant struggles and forms of life in Latin America while being attentive to differences in context at the same time?

FEDERICI: This is a discussion that is taking place in New York. People in the social movements who are inspired by the struggles in Latin America are now thinking in terms of territorial politics, the territory being a place where you have some form of collective control and even self-government. Clearly, the situation in the US is profoundly different. But thinking in terms of territory enables us to see that the neighborhoods in which we live are not neutral spaces, they are not just conglomerates of houses and people. They are very politically structured. In New York, for instance, since the '70s, there's been a process of "spatial deconcentration," whereby every neighborhood has been studied by local and federal authorities to figure out how to better control the movement of people and guarantee that the wrong people do not go to certain neighborhoods. Subway lines, bus lines, playgrounds have been restructured to make sure that poor people cannot easily go to places of wealth.

So looking at our neighborhoods as "territories" in this case means recognizing those factors of tension, of crisis, those power relations that traverse them that divide people but can also bring them together. The social centers that have opened in recent years in New York are attempting to do that, trying to engage in practices that create "territory," that is, create forms of aggregation. Building more collective forms of reproduction is a key aspect of this process. It is indispensable if we want to create "communities of resistance," spaces where people are connected and can engage in some collective decision-making.

NICK AND CARLA: Maybe one thing to follow up on this. In that question you talked about the forgotten impacts of really subtle things like architecture, planning, and in *Caliban and the Witch* you talk about the forgotten impacts of the witch hunts and how those impacts are still with us today. Are there underappreciated movements of joy and transformation where we haven't fully appreciated the impacts?

FEDERICI: There are so many movements. The suffragette movement, for example, is always portrayed as a bourgeois movement, but I'm discovering that it had a working-class dimension as well. But rather than thinking of particular movements, what most matters is discovering and re-creating the collective memory of past struggles. In the US there is a systematic attempt to destroy this memory, and now this is extending across the world, with the destruction of the main historical centers of the Middle East—a form of dispossession that has major consequences and yet is rarely discussed. Reviving the memory of the struggles of the past makes us feel part of something larger than our individual lives, and in this way it gives a new meaning to what we are doing and gives us courage, because it makes us less afraid of what can happen to us individually.

NICK AND CARLA: Another thing that we wanted to talk to you about is the style and tone of intellectual engagement. Your style is so generous, and you have a really militant critique of capitalism, but you're always pointing to examples in a range of different movements, and you seem to reserve really pointed attacks for large destructive institutions like the World Bank. It seems to us that this differs from a lot of radical critique today, which can be very focused on exposing complicities or limitations, talking about the ways that movements are lacking, that they haven't yet reached this or that, as well as targeting individuals. So we wanted to ask: Is this style something that you've cultivated and that you're intentional about, and maybe more generally, can you talk about the potential of theory in intellectual work today, and what joyful theory might look like? What makes theory enabling and transformative, and what gets in the way of that?

FEDERICI: It's partially a consequence of growing old. You understand things that when you're younger you didn't see. One thing that I've learned is to be more humble and to hold my judgment of people until I know them beyond what I can make out from what they say, realizing that people often say foolish things that they do not really believe or have not seriously thought about.

It also comes from recognizing that we can change, which means that we should stress our potential rather than our limits. One of the most amazing experiences in the women's movement was to see how much we could grow, learning to speak in public, write poetry, make beautiful posters. All this has given me a strong distaste for the impulse to squash everything at the first sign that something is not right.

I've made it a principle not to indulge in speech that is destructive. Striving to speak clearly, not to make people feel like fools because they don't understand what I say, is a good part of it. That's also something I've taken from the women's movement. So many times we had felt humiliated, being in situations where we didn't understand what men had said and didn't have the courage to ask what they meant. I don't want to make other people ever feel this way.

NICK AND CARLA: You're really good at that! One of the things we were talking about this morning is the question of identity, and a lot of the critiques of sad militancy that we have read really make identity into *the* problem quite a bit more than we would want to. We're trying to think through how to speak to the power of identity and experience while pointing to power of transformation and working across difference, and how the two of those aren't antithetical in the way they're sometimes set up, that they're crucial for each other.

FEDERICI: I think the critique of identity has taken on dimensions that are not always justified. What people often criticize as identity is actually the position that a person has had in the capitalist organization of work. For example, is being a housewife an identity? Yes, it's an identity, but it is also a particular place in the capitalist organization of work; like being a miner, it's also a particular form of exploitation. Identity is often used in a way that hides that exploitation. That's when it becomes problematic.

Moreover, behind identity there's also a history of struggle and resistance to exploitation. Identity can be a signpost for a whole history of struggle. When I say I am a feminist, for instance, I consciously connect myself to history of struggle that women have made. Identities can be mutable as well. "Woman," for example, is not a fixed identity. The concept of woman has undergone a tremendous change over the last fifty years.

The problem has been the wedding of "identity" with the politics of rights, as when we speak of women's rights, Indigenous peoples' rights, as if each group were entitled to a packet of entitlements but in isolation from each other, so that we lose sight of the commonalities and the possibility of a common struggle.

NICK AND CARLA: That's really helpful. Our last question is about hope. Spinoza himself is pretty wary of hope, but he sees it as quite future-oriented: to hope is also to fear, because you're attached to a future object or outcome. More generally hope is often equated with a naïve optimism: it can become fixated on a certain outcome. But in one of your interviews, you talked about it as something that's a lot more open-ended.[7] It's more the sense that we can do something. Do you think that hope is necessarily attached to a vision of the future?

FEDERICI: Hope is positive if it is an active passion but only if it does not replace the work necessary to make our action successful.

**

Silvia Federici is an Italian activist and author of many works, including *Caliban and the Witch* and *Revolution at Point Zero: Housework, Reproduction, and Feminist Struggle.* She was co-founder of the International Feminist Collective and organizer with the Wages for Housework Campaign in the '70s. She was a member of the Midnight Notes Collective.

Appendix 2: Breaking Down the Walls around Each Other—An Interview with Kelsey Cham C.

NICK AND CARLA: One of the things we're trying to think through with the notion of sad militancy is the way that Empire gets smuggled into radical movements in spaces through mistrust, fear, rigidity, shame, competition, and so on ... but we want to think this through without blaming individuals. It's not about individual feelings or behaviors; it's about ways of relating that are coming out of this system.

KELSEY: Yeah, we're re-creating it.

NICK AND CARLA: Yeah, and we're interested in talking to people that seem to be able to tap into something different, and I think you do that.

KELSEY: (laughs) I'm glad you think so.

NICK AND CARLA: I guess the first question is: does this resonate, does this description of sad militancy make sense to you?

Kelsey: Yeah, it's funny because I don't use those terms, but I find myself in situations where we're having conversations about the exact same things but with many different folks who are politically aware and trying to create change. It is really hard to not fall into sad militancy; I catch myself being overly critical of either myself or other people in their efforts to organize and create something better and new or something that's never been done before. It's frustrating, and I find myself asking "why is this happening, this constant critique?" It's totally internalized capitalist patriarchal shit.

I think it's connected to perfectionism and the desire to do things "the right way" that becomes a part of us—it's hard to not re-create that when that's how you grew up and have learned that this is what's true.

Nick and carla: So what do you think made you get to a place where you're able to catch yourself and do something else?

Kelsey: That's a really good question ... well, all those things are super isolating. Most people in this culture have experienced that pretty in-depth in their personal lives. I have, and when I'm critical of myself or other people, I try to strive for something that doesn't exist; I'm always unhappy and I get frustrated, I get angry. I can get violent ... those are things that aren't productive.

I don't know. I don't know if there's one specific thing; I don't even know if I'm very good at being joyfully militant or whatever. I think my background in karate has helped, though.... And basically recognizing that we're all in this together and we all have a common goal and making efforts to love each other—not just tolerate each other—but actually see how we can feel love for everyone to some degree. I think we're capable—maybe that's naïve or what-ever—but I think we're capable of doing that ... that's probably arguable too.

NICK AND CARLA: Do you think there are things that make rigidity or sad militancy spread?

KELSEY: Yeah for sure, I think people get sucked into stuff, right? I found myself going back to what's comfortable. If I'm part of a group and people start hating on a certain thing in a way, I think it's easy for me to get caught up in that. It's something that I try to catch myself doing and recognize that's not how I feel at all ... it's old patterns coming up again, and when you're in new situations it's easy for those patterns to come out.

NICK AND CARLA: Have you seen spaces, conversations, or practices shift from joyful militancy to sad militancy or vice versa?

KELSEY: Yes, I would say so. I think I've seen spaces where everything has ups and downs, and people have ups and downs—going from sad to joyful to sad again—it's exciting and then a key person leaves, or a project falls through, or maybe people are not happy with the way that everyone is contributing ... sometimes that energy falls or maybe people lose interest.

But sometimes I can shift the energy of an entire crew of people.... I find that usually when people are able to recognize that we're all in this together and it's not a battle against each other. I think that's usually what it is: having that foundation of common vision or goals or whatever. And usually there's someone who is able to be joyful.... In the same way that sad militancy is contagious, joy is also contagious; people get excited by new energy.

Nick and carla: What do you think encourages and sustains joyful militancy?

Kelsey: I dunno … I'm pretty new to this whole way of being, I guess, but I think humility is a huge part of it and also community credit—"we did that together"—and celebrating tiny accomplishments can be really awesome: celebrating each other's accomplishments and respecting that stuff. I think part of the sad militancy—just to go back to how it catches on—is because I think in our society we learn to be overly critical and perfectionist…. It's so easy to criticize people's work and what they're doing without recognizing what they're trying to do and what they're actually accomplishing. At the same time, criticism can be a gift for everyone involved when it's about learning and figuring things out together.

Nick and carla: So it's not even that criticism equals sad militancy; is there a way to do criticism that can be joyful?

Kelsey: Oh, totally. I was just talking about this with a friend the other day. I think it's important to talk to people about how they receive criticism and how they would want to, or if they even can safely, I guess. But for me I think it's really, really, really awesome when people give me feedback and constructive criticism in a respectful way; even if it's in a non-respectful way, I'll take it, I might be angry about it, it might make me irritable or hate on something, but I'll absorb it as well. All criticisms are gifts because they're perspectives that I probably didn't have before and I can work with. And I acknowledge that I can't make everyone happy and that's not what I'm trying to do. I want to be as inclusive as possible with the work that I'm doing, but there's no way that every single person is gonna be super stoked about it. And to receive criticism I also need to have a positive feedback system, where it's like: if I receive ten things I'm doing so-called "wrong," it will make me feel like I'm not doing anything right, and I don't know what to keep and what to change. It's like if you're playing cards and you think I'm just gonna fold and leave every time. But probably there are some things I should keep, so positive feedback is also really important.

CARLA AND NICK: We want to talk about the importance of trust, and the radical potential of trust, without turning trust into some commandment. Does this resonate? Can you talk about the potential of trusting folks up front and how you saw it play out at the Thistle?

KELSEY: Yeah, totally, I think that's awesome. Actually I think you [carla] were one of the first people to actually trust me without even knowing me. And I was like what the hell? Why? Why? How do you know I'm not gonna just fuck everything up and run away and steal a bunch of money and go? How do you know that? But in trusting me, I was like, holy shit: I trust this situation and this collective twenty times more, and I want to give back to it because I've been given this opportunity to do something that I've never been able to do before, which is awesome.

But I have been thinking about trust and how with trauma we build all these walls and we start to mistrust everything. I have a pretty hard time trusting people. There's a point where I'm like, this is too personal and too intimate and now my walls are going to go up. I was sitting and thinking about how ... probably one of the best ways to break down the walls of the system is to break down the walls around each other first, and I think that requires trust.

Joyful militancy and trust and compassion and humility are all tied together, I think: in other cultures, traditional cultures—I don't know a lot about this—but from what I know, older Indigenous cultures have these ideas of respect, humility, compassion, and I think in karate I've seen it, and it's interesting because karate is a martial art, a fighting tool, and one of the things that we learn is that we have to love everyone, including our opponents. And that's the toughest thing to say in this community. People are like "what the fuck, how can you say that, you can't just love your abuser." And it's true, I can't just let go of everything. It's not that; it's being compassionate, I think, to situations.

NICK AND CARLA: What makes it hard to nurture trust? What's been your experience with trust in your everyday? And in radical spaces?

KELSEY: I feel like trauma is the biggest hurdle for me. From what I see happening around me and my own self, a lot of people—not everyone—but a lot of people who are politically involved and radical are there because they're the short stick: they've been oppressed and traumatized. That's often what leads people to these ideas and values maybe? Well, for me that's true ... but I think when we lose trust in anything—either family or relationships or the system that we're part of—we build walls to protect ourselves. And it takes a lot of work to break down those walls, and we need to trust, and when you're trying to defend yourself all the time and you don't trust anything, it's like a sad circle—a catch-22—and that's what I've seen go on. It's not just about organizing in the community, it's not just about un-learning belief systems; it's also unlearning ways of being in ourselves, and that takes a lot of work and a lot of that shit nobody wants to look at or bring up again. And I know a lot of people are like, "this thing keeps coming up, and I'm blocking it because it's too scary." And I think that that's keeping us isolated and rigid.

CARLA AND NICK: So there's like a comfort and safety in remaining rigid, skeptical, untrusting?

KELSEY: There is! This whole world is based on fucking misery, and to be joyful is scary because it's kind of unknown. In capitalist systems, we're not meant to feel joy; I think it's about domination and power and gaining respect by taking part, but it has nothing to do with joy. Even now, I feel like people judge me for being too positive and too happy; people think I'm way younger than I am often because of my attitude; they're like "why aren't you bitter yet?" It's really interesting because it's scary to feel new things and not know where they're going to take you.

CARLA AND NICK: Can we have the expectation of trust up front? Do you think there's an alternative to the idea that trust always needs to be earned?

KELSEY: It's so hard in our society: you gotta earn everything; you earn money, you build trust, and respect. You gotta prove to me that I should trust you or respect you. And that's an interesting point; I have a tough time with that, trusting people. But I think it's a feedback system: prob-ably the more you allow yourself to trust people initially … the more well-reciprocated that will be. I felt it: you trusted me, and I didn't understand it. That's how fucked up our system is. Even though I didn't do anything wrong or to harm you, I didn't understand how someone could trust me without knowing me first.

NICK AND CARLA: There's this perception that all this stuff—trust, curiosity, uncertainty, joy—is naïve: if you're joyful or trusting you probably just don't understand what's going on or how bad things are. And with that, there's a perception that only people who are super privileged have the capacity to be joyful. How do you think about joyful militancy and trust in relation to privilege and oppression?

KELSEY: I think some of the most joyful people I've met are not coming from privileged backgrounds. I don't think it's true that only privileged people can be joyful. It's a blanket statement, and it's also kind of really oppressive and ignorant to say, I think. I think that's harsh for me to say, but I think that … a lot of people and friends that are coming from privileged backgrounds are some of the most rigid people and the most isolated. They don't feel at ease, and they're not comfortable, they're guilty. A lot of privilege makes it difficult to learn how to work cooperatively. But I've seen the effectiveness and power—I don't mean power like people who dominate—I mean power like the energy that comes from compassion and love and real collective work and humility. Humility's such a huge one.

It's part of our society to discount all that as naïve. Naïve is inexperience. What is inexperience? It comes from an ageist perspective: you're young, you only think like this because you're young; you haven't experienced enough. Actually some of the youngest people—kids—are often the most connected and able to absorb and create. It is ageist to associate joyfulness with naïveté. Maybe that's super harsh to say but I think it comes from our society's idea of what it means to be an adult, a youth, a child. Those systems are in place to keep us fuckin' stagnant and to keep kids stagnant and devalued and powerless.

CARLA AND NICK: Yeah, that's a useful way for us to think about it because it's easy to make all this into another set of norms: "just be this way." It's hard to talk about this in other ways, maybe because part of rigid militancy and activist-speak is constantly prescribing behaviors, and it's easy to hear joyful militancy as another prescription.

KELSEY: Maybe it's not a prescription, it is a practice.... I'm excited because I've been having these conversations with friends. I think it's really awesome that you're really intentionally introducing this. Because I think probably the amount of work it must have taken you (carla) to just start off trusting people is a fuck-load, probably.... and I'm realizing how important it is to share that ... Once we have something, we can share it with younger folks so that they don't have to go through the same struggles to get to these points. I feel like what I'm learning is probably at a way earlier stage in my life than when you probably learned it. And I'll be able to pass that on to the kids in my life when they're way younger, like four or five, starting to introduce these ideas, and they won't have to face the same struggles again, and we can go deeper, and it's exciting.

**

Kelsey Cham C. is a community organizer and settler of Chinese and Irish descent. Being involved with projects like the Purple Thistle has brought Kelsey depth and insight into trying to understand what the hell is going on in the world. Kelsey is focused on organizing experiential learning projects with youth and adults in gardening, mycology, fermentation, and "ki" (chi- based) karate.

Appendix 3: Further Reading

Though we have used direct quotes and endnotes as a way to acknowledge our intellectual debts and sources throughout the book, we often found ourselves wanting to include more of the currents and perspectives that have shaped this work. With that in mind, we have assembled some articles, zines, books, films, interviews, and stories for those who want to go further with some of the ideas explored in each chapter, providing links to online versions where possible. This list is diverse, and elements of these texts are in tension with each other and our own work, and we think they are all worth approaching in the spirit of critical and affirmative reading. We also recommend checking out work by everyone we interviewed and cited, and we are planning to create a fuller list on our website: joyfulmilitancy.com.

Chapter 1: Empire, Militancy, Joy

Amadahy, Zainab. *Wielding the Force: The Science of Social Justice,* Smashwords Edition, 2013 (non-fiction book).
Anonymous. "The Tyranny of Imagery, or, How to Escape the Zoopraxiscope," *Hostis* 2, (2016) (essay).

brown, adrienne maree and Walidah Imarisha, eds. *Octavia's Brood: Science Fiction Stories from Social Justice Movements*, AK Press 2015 (collected short fiction).

Colectivo Situaciones. "On the Researcher Militant," 2003 (essay), http://eipcp.net/transversal/0406/colectivosituaciones/en.

Federici, Silvia. *Caliban and the Witch: Women, the Body, and Primitive Accumulation,* Autonomedia, 2004 (non-fiction book).

Holloway, John. *Change the World without Taking Power,* Pluto Press, 2005 (non-fiction book).

Lorde, Audre. *Sister Outsider,* Crossing Press, 1984 (collected essays).

Massumi, Brian. "Navigating Movements" interviewed by Mary Zournazi, https://archive.org/stream/InterviewWithBrianMassumi/intmassumi_djvu.txt.

P. M. *bolo'bolo*, Autonomedia, 1985 (non-fiction book), http://sfbay-anarchists.org/wp-content/uploads/2015/04/bb_3.pdf.

Shukaitis, Stevphen. *Imaginal Machines: Autonomy & Self-Organization in the Revolutions of Everyday Life*, Minor Compositions, 2009 (non-fiction book), http://www.minorcompositions.info/wp-content/uploads/2009/10/ImaginalMachines-web.pdf.

Chapter 2: Friendship, Freedom, Ethics

Alfred, Taiaiake. *Wasase: Indigenous Pathways of Action and Freedom,* University of Toronto Press, 2005 (non-fiction book).

Anonymous. "Robot Seals as Counter-Insurgency: Friendship and Power from Aristotle to Tiqqun (blog post), https://human-strike.wordpress.com/2013/08/27/robot-seals-as-counter-insurgency-friendship-and-power-from-aristotle-to-tiqqun/.

Day, Richard. *Gramsci Is Dead: Anarchist Currents in the Newest Social Movements,* Between the Lines, 2005 (non-fiction book).

Ferrante, Elena. *My Brilliant Friend,* Europa, 2012 (novel).

Knowing the Land Is Resistance. "Towards an Anarchist Ecology" (blog post/zine), https://knowingtheland.com/2014/01/28/new-zine-collecting-towards-and-anarchist-ecology/.

Mies, Maria. *Patriarchy and Accumulation on a World Scale: Women in the International Division of Labour*, Zed Books, 2014 (non-fiction book).

Simpson, Leanne Betasamosake. "Decolonial Love: Building Resurgent Communities of Connection," 2014 (video recorded talk), http://emmatalks.org/session/leanne-simpson.

Walia, Harsha. "Decolonizing Together," *Briarpatch*, 2012 (essay), https://briarpatchmagazine.com/articles/view/decolonizing-together

Yalom, Irvin. *The Spinoza Problem: A Novel,* Basic Books, 2013 (novel).

Chapter 3: Trust and Responsibility as Common Notions

bergman, carla, and Corin Brown. *Common Notions: Handbook Not Required.* 2015 (documentary).

Esteva, Gustavo, and Madhu Suri Prakash, *Grassroots Post-Modernism: Remaking the Soil of Cultures*, Zed Books, 1998 (non-fiction book).

Hern, Matt. *Everywhere all the Time: A New Deschooling Reader*. AK Press, 2008 (non-fiction anthology).

Holloway, John. "Greece: Hope Drowns in the Reality of a Dying World, or Does it?" (video lecture), http://www.johnholloway.com.mx/2015/10/05/greecehope-drowns-in-the-reality-of-a-dying-world-or-does-it.

Imarisha, Walidah. *Angels with Dirty Faces: Three Stories of Crime, Prison, and Redemption*, AK Press, 2016 (creative non-fiction).

The Invisible Committee. *To Our Friends*, Semiotext(e), 2015 (non-fiction book), https://theanarchistlibrary.org/library/the-invisible-committe-to-our-friends.

Killjoy, Margaret. "Take What You Need and Compost the Rest: an introduction to post-civilized theory," Strangers in a Tangled Wilderness, 2010 (zine), http://www.tangledwilderness.org/take-what-you-need-and-compost-the-rest/.

Kimmerer, Robin Wall. *Braiding Sweetgrass*, Milkweed, 2015 (non-fiction book).

Law, Victoria. "Against Carceral Feminism," *Jacobin,* 2014 (essay), https://www.jacobinmag.com/2014/10/against-carceral-feminism.

Simpson, Leanne, ed. *Lighting the Eighth Fire: The Liberation, Resurgence, and Protection of Indigenous Nations*, Arbeiter Ring, 2008 (non-fiction anthology).

Zibechi, Raúl. *Dispersing Power: Social Movements as Anti-State Forces*, 2010 (non-fiction book).

Chapter 4: Stifling Air, Burnout, Political Performance

Debord, Guy. *The Society of the Spectacle*, 1967 (non-fiction book) https://www.marxists.org/reference/archive/debord/society.htm.

Foucault, Michel. "Preface," in Gilles Deleuze and Felix Guattari, *Anti-Oedipus: Capitalism and Schizophrenia*, 1972 (non-fiction book).

Freeman, Jo. "Trashing: the Dark Side of Sisterhood," 1976 (essay), http://www.jofreeman.com/joreen/trashing.htm.

INCITE! Women of Color Against Violence, eds., *The Revolution Will Not be Funded: Beyond the Non-Profit Industrial Complex*, South End Press, 2009 (non-fiction anthology).

Institute for Precarious Consciousness, *We Are All Very Anxious*, 2014 (zine), https://cloudfront.crimethinc.com/pdfs/We-Are-All-Very-Anxious.pdf.

Nietzsche, Friedrich. *On the Genealogy of Morality*, 1887 (non-fiction book), http://www.inp.uw.edu.pl/mdsie/Political_Thought/GeneologyofMorals.pdf.

X, Andrew. "Give Up Activism," 2009 (essay/zine), https://theanarchistlibrary.org/library/andrew-x-give-up-activism.

Chapter 5: Undoing Rigid Radicalism

Ahmad, Asam. "A Note on Call-Out Culture," *Briarpatch,* 2015 (essay), https://briarpatchmagazine.com/articles/view/a-note-on-call-out-culture.

C., Kelsey Cham. "Radical Language in the Mainstream,"
    Perspectives on Anarchist Theory 29, 2016 (es-
    say), https://anarchiststudies.org/2017/03/09/
    radical-language-in-the-mainstream-by-kelsey-cham-c.

CrimethInc., "Against Ideology?," 2010 (essay), http://www.cri-
    methinc.com/texts/atoz/ideology.php.

crow, scott. "In a Moving River Nothing Can Ever Be Set
    in Stone: A Letter for Insurgent Dreamers," (essay) in
    Emergency Hearts, Molotov Dreams, GTK Press, 2015,
    https://theanarchistlibrary.org/library/scott-crow-in-a-
    moving-river-nothing-can-ever-be-set-in-stone-a-letter-for-
    insurgent-dreamers.

Foucault, Michel. "Preface," in Gilles Deleuze and Felix Guattari,
    Anti-Oedipus: Capitalism and Schizophrenia, Viking Press,
    1977, http://cnqzu.com/library/Philosophy/Deleuze,%20
    Gilles%20and%20Felix%20Guattari-AntiOedipus.pdf.

Heckert, Jamie. "Anarchy and Opposition," (essay) In *Queering
    Anarchism: Addressing and Undressing Power and Desire*,
    AK Press, 2012.

Sedgwick, Eve Kosofsky. "Paranoid Reading and Reparative
    Reading, or, You're so Paranoid, You Probably Think This
    Essay Is about You" (essay), in *Touching Feeling: Affect,
    Pedagogy, Performativity*, Duke University Press, 2003,
    https://sydney.edu.au/arts/slam/downloads/documents/
    novel_studies/3_Sedgwick.pdf.

Shotwell, Alexis. *Against Purity: Living Ethically in Compromised
    Times*, University of Minnesota Press, 2016 (non-fiction
    book).

starr, amory. "Grumpywarriorcool: What Makes Our Movements
    White?" (essay), in *Igniting a Revolution: Voices in Defense of*

the Earth, AK Press, 2006, http://trabal.org/texts/grumpy-warriorcool.pdf.

Thoburn, Nicholas. "Weatherman, the Militant Diagram, and the Problem of Political Passion," *New Formations* 68, 2009 (academic article), http://sfbay-anarchists.org/wp-content/uploads/2014/01/Thoburn-Weatherman-the-Militant-Diagram-and-the-Problem-of-Political-Passion.pdf.

Glossary of Terms

ACTIVE

Joyful passions give us clues about becoming active in the growth of joy, opening the potential for tuning into, stoking, amplifying, modulating, and tending to emergent powers. To become active in joyful transformation is to become capable of participating in the forces that increase one's capacity to affect and be affected. To become capable of feeling and doing new things always requires an openness and vulnerability, and active participation requires a capacity to sustain this openness to change. The desire for full control or independence remains trapped in passivity, because learning to participate in joy's unfolding means being partially undone and transformed through an open-ended, uncontrollable process.

AFFECT

Affect is at the heart of Spinoza's philosophy of a "world in the making," in which things are defined not by what they *are* but by what they *do:* how they affect and are affected. To attend to affect means becoming attuned to the relations and encounters that compose us, right here and right now. To be affected intensely won't feel straightforwardly good or happy because intense affects are what transform, undo, and remake us. Emotions are a capturing of affect—a way of registering *some* of the forces that compose us. There can be no handbook for affect, because each encounter— each transition we undergo—is unique. No one knows what a body is capable of, and one only learns by experimenting: by *becoming* capable of new things. The capacity to affect and be affected leads to questions at the heart of this book: How do we affect each other? How can we become more capable, attuned, and alive together? What gets in the way of all this, and how might some of these obstacles be affective: intertwined with our comfort, safety, happiness, habits and pleasures?

AFFINITY

The notion of affinity that we draw on comes from anarchism but stretches beyond the "affinity group" in which people who trust each other get together for a particular action. Organizing and connecting by affinity is an alternative (and sometimes a complement) to organizing on the basis of preexisting ideologies, identities, and interests. It basically means encountering each other and seeing how it goes, searching for something shared that is emergent rather than preexisting. It orients us to the question of what we *might be able to do together* rather than (only) *who* we are and what we *should* do. To find affinity, in this sense, is not about finding people who are "like us" or who we "like" but about searching out connections and alliances through which we increase our powers and capacities.

COMMON NOTIONS

Common notions are not fixed ideas but shared thinking-feeling-doings that support joyful transformation. As such, they require uncertainty, experimentation, and flexibility amid changing circumstances, and they exist in tension with fixed systems of morality and ideology. Common notions are processes through which people figure things out together and become active in joy's unfolding, learning to participate in and sustain new capacities. We suggest that trust and responsibility can be emergent and relational common notions rather than fixed duties. In a certain way, common notions are fragile: if they are turned into fixed ways of doing things or moral commandments, detached from the ethical responsiveness that animated them, they die.

CONVIVIALITY

To undo Empire's radical monopolies entails participating in convivial forms of life: assemblages of tools, feelings, infrastructures habits, skills, and relationships that enable and support the flourishing of creativity, autonomy, collective responsibility, and struggle. Conviviality gets at the way in which people are able to figure out things for themselves, from transformative justice that undoes dependence on cops and courts, to regenerative forms of subsistence that support a diversity of nonhuman critters, to alternatives to school that enable intergenerational learning, to all of the innumerable ways that people are reviving and inventing ways of living and dying that break Empire's monopoly over life today.

DESCHOOLING

We use "deschooling" in two different ways. The act of deschooling is a process whereby a previously schooled person learns to shed habits and behaviors inculcated through schooling. "Deschooling" is also used to describe the creation of alternatives to schools and institutionalized education by generating learning environments that work from nonhierarchical relationships between learners and mentors. This means recognizing that we are always learning, everywhere, and that sharing knowledge works in all directions and relationships (a child can teach an adult, and so on).

EMPIRE

Empire is the name for the organized catastrophe in which we live today. It is not really an "it" but a tangle of habits, tendencies, and apparatuses that sustain exploitation and control. We argue that it entrenches and accumulates sadness: it crushes and co-opts forces of transformation and detaches people from their own powers and capacities. It keeps us passive, stuck in forms of life in which everything is done to us or for us. This takes place through overt violence and repression, and the entrenchment of hierarchical divisions like heteropatriarchy and racism, by inducing dependence on institutions and markets and by affective control and subjection.

ETHICS

We suggest that ethics—and ethical attunement—is an enabling alternative to morality. Ethics is a space that lies beyond morality *and* an anything-goes relativism. This conception runs against the grain of many standard definitions of ethics that basically conceive it as an individual version of morality (ethical consumption, ethical principles, and other rules to live by). Rather than a fixed set of principles, ethics means becoming attuned to the complexity of the world and our immersion in it. It means actively working on and reshaping relationships, cultivating some ties and severing others, and figuring out how to do without the fixed rules of ideology or morality. It entails the capacity for responsibility, not as a fixed duty but as *response-ability*—the capacity to be responsive to relationships and encounters. Compared to morality, ethics entails *more* fidelity to our relations in their immediacy—to all the forces that compose us and affect us—not less.

FORMS OF LIFE

The concept of a "form of life" is borrowed from Tiqqun, and we have used it synonymously with "worlds," without unpacking it rigorously, in favor of focusing on other concepts. Every form of life has an affective and ethical consistency. A form of life is irreducible to the people, practices, desires, and feelings that compose it—inseparable from the way people feel, from the questions they have, from their subtle gestures, from the place where they live and the nonhuman elements there. Forms of life are not stable units that can be represented with precision, with a fixed inside and outside; instead, they are patterned relations in movement. In this sense, the concept of a form of life orients us to the texture of life here and now. The forms of life proper to Empire are characterized by a paradoxical attenuation of intensity and joy—the very things that subtend forms of life. Empire's apparatuses of subjection nurture an attenuated form of life in which desire is turned against itself and subjects remain stuck in loops of anxiety, dependence, fear, evaluation, and categorization. One cannot imagine oneself into a different form of life or plan it out. Connecting with other forms of life entails entanglement with transformative capacities and the values, penchants, and relations that go along with them. These other affective worlds are always in the making in the cracks of Empire: people are inventing and recovering ways of living and relating that are joyful and transformative, through which they are exploring new capacities together.

FREEDOM

Freedom means finding the transformative potential in our own situations and relationships. This is very different from conventional, Western, patriarchal definitions of freedom, which tend to conceive it as a state of being un-inhibited, unaffected, unhindered. This "free" individual of Empire is a form of subjection invented by capitalism and the state, enclosing us in a trap of market-mediated choices, contracts, and the refinement of our individual preferences. From the relational perspective we are advo-cating, freedom cannot be an escape from all connections and relations or any destination; it can only mean find-ing room to move in the present. Finding the wiggle room of freedom is joyful: a collective increase in capacity to work on relationships. It is in this sense that we argue that friendship and kinship are the basis of freedom: intimate, durable, fierce bonds with others that undo us, remake us, and create new capacities together.

IDEOLOGY

In the broad sense that we use it here, "ideology" means having a preexisting set of answers for political ques-tions. This can be a capitalist ideology that sees every-thing in terms of individual preferences and self-interest or a Marxist ideology that evaluates everything in terms of whether or not it will lead to a workers' revolution or any other perspective that uses a fixed system of thought to evaluate and manage encounters. By sorting unfold-ing events into categories, everything becomes recogniz-able, and thus one is closed off from the capacity to be affected intensely and transformed. To be transformed by an encounter, in contrast, is to be affected in a way that is disorienting and undoes some of the habits, categories, and perceptions enabled by ideology. To undo ideology requires a kind of *thinking-feeling* that is relatively open and vulnerable.

JOY

From Spinoza, joy means an increase in a body's capacity to affect and be affected. It means becoming capable of feeling or doing something new; it is not just a subjective feeling but a real event that takes place. In this sense it is different from happiness, which is one of many potential ways a body might turn joy into a subjective experience. This increase in capacity is a process of transformation, and it might feel scary, painful, and exhilarating, but it will always be more than just the emotions one feels about it. It is the growth of shared power to do, feel, and think *more*.

MILITANCY

We want to revalue militancy as fierce conviction in which struggle and care, fierceness and tenderness, go hand in hand. This emergent militancy is enabled by supportive and transformative relationships, which undo the stultifying forms of subjection inculcated by Empire. This is different from the militancy associated with strains of Marxism-Leninism, Maoism, and other currents that historically have been criticized for machismo, coldness, and vanguardism. At the same time, there are nascent tendencies of joyful militancy everywhere, including movements associated with rigidity. As something that comes out of and depends on relationships, joyful militancy is not a fixed perspective or an ideal to aspire to, but also a lived process of transformative struggle.

MORALITY

Morality is the fixing of a division between good and evil that is divorced from the intense uniqueness or singularity of situations, and the potentials therein. As such, it is a form of subjection that divorces us from our ability to be responsive to changing conditions, offering up rigid divisions between good and evil. We focus in particular on the rise of a *liberal* morality inherited from Christianity, which upholds the status quo and constantly regulates and pathologizes resistance and otherness. We suggest that an *anti-liberal, radical* morality has grown in reaction, attempting to turn the tables by pathologizing Empire and rooting out any form of complicity with it. This is a poisonous trap: anti-liberal morality purports to be against Empire, but it smuggles in penchants for guilt, shame, and self-righteousness, leading to new forms of radical policing and regulation in radical movements and spaces.

PASSIVE

Much of the time, bodies undergo joy and sadness *passively*: we are always being affected by forces to which we are not attuned. To be affected passively is to undergo waves of joy and sadness (passions) without being able to participate in the process. One might experience a surge of joy and then suddenly lose the connection to those forces, without having much of a sense of what made the surge possible or what led to its end. Sadness (the reduction of capacities) is always passive, but bodies can become active in and through joy.

RADICAL MONOPOLY

"Radical monopoly" is Ivan Illich's term to get at the ways that modern institutions and infrastructures—from schools to courts to hospitals to highways—have made us dependent on them by monopolizing life and forcing out alternatives. In so-called "developed" countries in particular, the growth of modern institutions and industrial tools have created a form of life that is increasingly dependent on expert knowledge and industrial production. Through these monopolies, the skills, practices, and relationships that sustained grassroots, convivial forms of dying have been subjugated and in some cases completely annihilated. We take this a bit further by arguing that contemporary societies of control tend increasingly towards an affective monopoly, suffusing our habits, desires, and tendencies through perpetual surveillance, stimulation, and individualization.

SADNESS

Sadness is the reduction of one's capacity to affect and be affected. It is not necessarily about feeling unhappy or despairing but about the ways that a body loses capacities, becoming more closed-off or inhibited. Because we found it is so easily conflated with sorrow, we tend to use words like "stifling," "stultifying," "depleting," "deadening," and "numbing" to get at the affections of sadness. Sadness can never be escaped or avoided completely; all things wax, wane, and change.

SUBJECTION

"Subjection" gets at the ways that power does not merely oppress its subjects from above but composes and creates them. People are not simply being tricked into participating in Empire's stifling forms of life, nor are we "choosing" to do so, as if we could simply opt out. On the contrary, under certain sets of conditions, people can be made to desire fascism, repression, and violence even if these forces are killing them. This form of power cannot simply be opposed because it is the condition of our existence; it is part of who we are and what we want, and our habits and pleasures have been shaped by it. For example, the promise of happiness through consumption can make us chase after experiences or objects that deplete us even though they are pleasurable, closing off our capacity to be affected otherwise. In a different way, social media train their subjects into perpetual performance of an online identity, and the anxious management of our profiles closes us off from other forms of connection. Rigid radicalism induces a hypervigilant search for mistakes and flaws, stifling the capacity for experimentation. None of these modes of subjection dictate how exactly subjects will behave; instead they generate tendencies or attractor points that pull subjects into predictable, stultifying orbits. Resisting or transforming these systems is never straightforward, because it means resisting and transforming one's own habits and desires. It means surprising both the structure and oneself with something unexpected, new, and enabling.

Notes

Introduction

1 Audre Lorde, *Sister Outsider: Essays and Speeches* (Berkeley: Crossing Press, 1984), 4.

2 Raoul Vaneigem, *The Revolution of Everyday Life*, trans. Donald Nicholson-Smith (Seattle: Rebel Press, 2001), 26.

3 Michel Foucault, "Preface," in *Anti-Oedipus: Capitalism and Schizophrenia*, by Gilles Deleuze and Félix Guattari (Minneapolis: University of Minnesota Press, 1983), xi–xiv.

4 The concept of the "public secret" originated with situationism, and we borrow it from the Institute of Precarious Consciousness, in their suggestion that anxiety is a public secret of contemporary capitalism. See Institute for Precarious Consciousness, "Anxiety, Affective Struggle, and Precarity Consciousness-Raising," *Interface* 6, no. 2 (2014), 271–300.

5 Alfredo M. Bonanno, *Armed Joy* (London: Elephant Editions, 1998), https://theanarchistlibrary.org/library/alfredo-m-bonanno-armed-joy.

6 See, for instance John Holloway, *Change the World without*

Taking Power: The Meaning of Revolution Today (London: Pluto Press, 2005), 19–42; Invisible Committee, *To Our Friends* 216–19.

7 BIPOC is an acronym for Black, Indigenous, and People of Color. We understand these not as ethnic categories or essentialist identities but instead complex political categories forged in struggles against white supremacy and settler colonialism. For instance, the creation of BIPOC-specific spaces or "caucuses" within various struggles has created opportunities for understanding how racism or whiteness is playing out and how it can be confronted effectively.

8 The concept of sad militancy comes to us from Michel Foucault and Colectivo Situaciones. See Foucault, "Preface"; Colectivo Situaciones, "Something More on Research Militancy: Footnotes on Procedures and (In)Decisions," in *Constituent Imagination*, ed. Stevphen Shukaitis, Erika Biddle and David Graeber (Oakland: AK Press, 2007), 73–93.

Chapter One

1 Brian Massumi, "Translator's Foreword: Pleasures of Philosophy," in *A Thousand Plateaus: Capitalism and Schizophrenia*, by Gilles Deleuze and Félix Guattari (Minneapolis: University of Minnesota Press, 1987), ix–xv.

2 Zainab Amadahy, "Protest Culture: How's It Working for Us?," *Rabble.ca*, July 20, 2010, http://rabble.ca/news/2010/07/protest-culture-how%E2%80%99s-it-working-us.

3 This phrase is often attributed to Frederic Jameson, who wrote, "Someone once said that it is easier to imagine the end of the world than to imagine the end of capitalism." See Frederic Jameson, "Future City," *New Left Review* 21 (2003), 77.

4 Gilles Deleuze and Félix Guattari, *Anti-Oedipus: Capitalism and Schizophrenia* (Minneapolis: University of Minnesota Press, 1983), 38.

5 Audre Lorde, *Sister Outsider* (Trumansburg, NY: Crossing Press, 1984), 53.

6 "The Wild Beyond: With and for the Undercommons," in *The Undercommons: Fugitive Planning & Black Study*, by Fred Moten and Stefano Harney (Wivenhoe: Minor Compositions, 2013), 10, http://www.minorcompositions.info/wp-content/uploads/2013/04/undercommons-web.pdf.

7 Gilles Deleuze and Claire Parnet, *Dialogues II* (New York: Columbia University Press, 2007), 61.

8 Dean Spade, "On *Normal Life*," interview by Natalie Oswin, *Society and Space* (January 2014), http://societyandspace.org/2014/01/15/on-6/.

9 "Joy—Definition of Joy in English," *Oxford English Dictionary* (Oxford: Oxford University Press, 2016), https://en.oxforddictionaries.com/definition/joy.

10 Rebecca Solnit, "We Could Be Heroes," EMMA Talks, Vancouver, February 17, 2016, http://emmatalks.org/session/rebecca-solnit/.

11 Sara Ahmed, *The Promise of Happiness* (Durham: Duke University Press, 2010), 192.

12 Leanne Betasamosake Simpson, "Indict the System: Indigenous and Black Connected Resistance," LeanneSimpson.ca, http://leannesimpson.ca/indict-the-system-indigenous-black-connected-resistance.

13 Our interpretation of Spinoza's concept of joy comes from many sources, but one of the most helpful is Mary Zournazi's interview with the affect theorist Brian Massumi, in which he

distinguishes joy from happiness. See Mary Zournazi, "Navigating Movements: A Conversation with Brian Massumi," in *Hope: New Philosophies for Change* (New York: Routledge, 2002), 241–242.

14 Gustavo Esteva, interview by carla bergman and Nick Montgomery, email, April 26, 2014.

15 Silvia Federici, interview by carla bergman and Nick Montgomery, telephone, January 18, 2016.

16 Lorde, *Sister Outsider*, 57.

17 adrienne maree brown, interview by Nick Montgomery and carla bergman, email, November 11, 2015.

18 This reading of Deleuze is indebted to conversations with Kim Smith and the reading she has developed of Susan Ruddick. See Susan Ruddick, "The Politics of Affect: Spinoza in the Work of Negri and Deleuze," *Theory, Culture & Society* 27, no. 4 (2010), 21–45.

19 Bædan, "The Anti-Social Turn," *Bædan: Journal of Queer Nihilism* 1 (August 2012), 186.

20 This notion of wisdom is drawn from Claire Carlisle's helpful explanation of Spinozan wisdom as something akin to "emotional intelligence." See Claire Carlisle, "Spinoza, Part 7: On the Ethics of the Self," *Guardian*, March 21, 2011, https://www.theguardian.com/commentisfree/belief/2011/mar/21/spinoza-ethics-of-the-self.

21 Marina Sitrin, interview by Nick Montgomery and carla bergman, email, February 4, 2016.

22 "Militant," *Wikipedia*, https://en.wikipedia.org.

23 ISIL stands for the Islamic State of Iraq and the Levant, often used interchangeably with Islamic State of Iraq and Syria (ISIS).

24 Melanie Matining, interview by carla bergman and Nick

Montgomery, in person, May 6, 2014.

25 Jackie Wang, "Against Innocence: Race, Gender and the Politics of Safety," *LIES Journal* 1 (2012), 13.

26 Ibid., 10.

27 Glen Coulthard, interview by carla bergman and Nick Montgomery, in person, March 16, 2016.

28 Ibid.

29 Kiera L. Ladner and Leanne Simpson, eds., *This Is an Honour Song: Twenty Years since the Blockades* (Winnipeg: Arbeiter Ring, 2010), 1.

30 Deborah B. Gould, *Moving Politics: Emotion and ACT UP's Fight against AIDS* (Chicago: University of Chicago Press, 2009), 178.

31 Sebastián Touza, interview by Nick Montgomery and carla bergman, email, February 2, 2016.

32 Sebastián Touza, "Antipedagogies for Liberation Politics, Consensual Democracy and Post-Intellectual Interventions" (PhD dissertation, Simon Fraser University, 2008), 136–37. https://www.academia.edu/544417/Antipedagogies_for_liberation_politics_consensual_democracy_and_post-intellectual_interventions.

33 For a fuller discussion of these dynamics, see Marina Sitrin, *Everyday Revolutions: Horizontalism and Autonomy in Argentina* (London: Zed Books, 2012).

34 Margaret Killjoy, interview by carla bergman and Nick Montgomery, email, March 8, 2014.

Chapter 2: Friendship, Freedom, Ethics, Affinity

1 Anonymous, "Robot Seals as Counter-Insurgency:

Friendship and Power from Aristotle to Tiqqun," *Human Strike*, https://humanstrike.wordpress.com/2013/08/27/robot-seals-as-counter-insurgency-friendship-and-power-from-aristotle-to-tiqqun.

2 brown, interview by Nick Montgomery and carla bergman.

3 The turn of phrase "making kin" comes to us from the feminist philosopher Donna Haraway. See Donna Haraway, "Anthropocene, Capitalocene, Plantationocene, Chthulucene: Making Kin," *Environmental Humanities* 6/1 (2015), 161.

4 Ibid., 163.

5 "Freedom—Definition of Freedom in English," *Oxford English Dictionary* (Oxford: Oxford University Press, 2016). https://en.oxforddictionaries.com/definition/freedom.

6 Douglas Harper, "Free (Adj.)," *Online Etymology Dictionary*, http://www.etymonline.com.

7 Ibid.

8 American Heritage Dictionaries, eds., *Word Histories and Mysteries: From Abracadabra to Zeus* (Boston: Houghton Mifflin, 2004), 103.

9 Invisible Committee, *To Our Friends*, trans. Robert Hurley (South Pasadena, CA: Semiotext(e), 2015), 127.

10 Thomas Hobbes, *Leviathan* (Oxford: Oxford Paperbacks, 2008), chap. 13.

11 This short account of the Age of Reason is drawn primarily from Silvia Federici. See Federici, *Caliban and the Witch: Women, the Body and Primitive Accumulation* (New York: Autonomedia, 2004), 133–62.

12 Some books we have found helpful include Jane Bennett, *Vibrant Matter: A Political Ecology of Things* (Durham: Duke University Press, 2010); Gilles Deleuze, *Expressionism in*

Philosophy: Spinoza, trans. Martin Joughin (New York: Zone Books, 1992); Moira Gatens, ed., *Feminist Interpretations of Benedict Spinoza* (University Park: Penn State University Press, 2009); Antonio Negri, *The Savage Anomaly: The Power of Spinoza's Metaphysics and Politics* (Minneapolis: University of Minnesota Press, 1991); Tiqqun, *Introduction to Civil War*, trans. Alexander R. Galloway and Jason E. Smith (Los Angeles: Semiotext(e), 2010).

13 Our reading of Spinoza is drawn primarily from Deleuze and those he has influenced. For helpful introductions to this lineage, see Gilles Deleuze, "Lecture on Spinoza's Concept of Affect" (Lecture, Cours Vincennes, Paris, 1978), https://www.gold.ac.uk/media/deleuze_spinoza_affect.pdf; Michael Hardt, "The Power to Be Affected," *International Journal of Politics, Culture, and Society* 28/3 (September 1, 2015), 215–22; Brian Massumi, *Politics of Affect* (Cambridge: Polity, 2015).

14 "Ethics—Definition of Ethics in English," *Oxford English Dictionary* (Oxford: Oxford University Press, 2016), https://en.oxforddictionaries.com/definition/ethics.

15 Deleuze, "Lecture on Spinoza's Concept of Affect."

16 This anecdote is based on conversations and exchanges with Kim Smith.

17 Invisible Committee, *The Coming Insurrection* (Los Angeles: Semiotext(e), 2009), 32.

18 Haraway, "Anthropocene, Capitalocene, Plantationocene, Chthulucene."

19 Ivan Illich to Madhu Suri Prakash, "Friendship," n.d.

20 This is drawn from Anonymous, "Robot Seals as Counter-Insurgency."

21 Coulthard, interview by carla bergman and Nick Montgomery.

22 See for instance Maria Mies, *Patriarchy and Accumulation on a World Scale: Women in the International Division of Labour* (London: Zed Books, 2014); Andrea Smith, "Heteropatriarchy and the Three Pillars of White Supremacy: Rethinking Women of Colour Organizing," in *The Color of Violence: The Incite! Anthology*, INCITE! Women of Color Against Violence, eds., (Cambridge, MA: South End Press, 2006), 66–73; Andrea Smith, *Conquest: Sexual Violence and American Indian Genocide* (Cambridge, MA: South End Press, 2005); Federici, *Caliban and the Witch*.

23 Silvia Federici, "Preoccupying: Silvia Federici," interview by Occupied Times, October 25, 2014, http://theoccupiedtimes. org/?p=13482.

24 Dean Spade, "For Lovers and Fighters," in *We Don't Need Another Wave: Dispatches from the Next Generation of Feminists*, ed. Melody Berger (Emeryville: Seal Press, 2006), 28–39, http://www.makezine.enoughenough.org/newpoly2.html.

25 bell hooks, *Outlaw Culture: Resisting Representations* (New York: Routledge, 2006), 249.

26 Leanne Betasamosake Simpson, "I Am Not a Nation-State," *Indigenous Nationhood Movement*, November 6, 2013, http://nationsrising.org/i-am-not-a-nation-state.

27 Leanne Betasamosake Simpson, interview by Nick Montgomery and carla bergman, email, November 2, 2015.

28 Raúl Zibechi, *Territories in Resistance: A Cartography of Latin American Social Movements*, trans. Ramor Ryan (Oakland: AK Press, 2012), 39.

29 Ibid., 41.

30 Silvia Federici, "Permanent Reproductive Crisis: An Interview with Silvia Federici," interview by Marina Vishmidt,

July 3, 2013, http://www.metamute.org/editorial/articles/
permanent-reproductive-crisis-interview-silvia-federici.

31 Mia Mingus, "On Collaboration: Starting
with Each Other," *Leaving Evidence*, August 3, 2012,
https://leavingevidence.wordpress.com/2012/08/03/
on-collaboration-starting-with-each-other.

32 Gustav Landauer, *Revolution and Other Writings: A
Political Reader*, ed. Gabriel Kuhn (Oakland: PM Press, 2010),
214.

33 Ibid., 90.

34 Ibid., 101.

35 Ibid., 91.

36 scott crow, *Black Flags and Windmills: Hope, Anarchy,
and the Common Ground Collective*, 2nd ed. (Oakland: PM Press,
2014), 199.

37 Richard J. F. Day, *Gramsci Is Dead: Anarchist Currents
in the Newest Social Movements* (Toronto: Between the Lines,
2005), 127.

38 Richard J. F. Day, "From Hegemony to Affinity," *Cultural
Studies* 18/5 (2004), 716–48.

39 Subcomandante Insurgente Marcos, *Ya Basta! Ten Years of
the Zapatista Uprising*, ed. Ziga Vodovnik (Oakland: AK Press,
2004), 77.

40 Gloria Anzaldúa, "(Un)natural Bridges, (Un)safe Spaces,"
in *This Bridge We Call Home: Radical Visions for Transformation*,
Gloria Anzaldúa and AnaLouise Keating, eds. (New York:
Routledge, 2002), 3.

41 Zainab Amadahy, "Community, 'Relationship
Framework' and Implications for Activism," *Rabble.
ca*, July 13, 2010, http://rabble.ca/news/2010/07/

community-%E2%80%98relationship-framework%E2%80%99-
and-implications-activism.

42 Coulthard, interview by carla bergman and Nick
Montgomery.

43 Glen Sean Coulthard, *Red Skin, White Masks: Rejecting
the Colonial Politics of Recognition* (Minneapolis: University of
Minnesota Press, 2014), 31.

44 Coulthard, interview by carla bergman and Nick
Montgomery.

45 Leanne Simpson, *Dancing on Our Turtle's Back: Stories
of Nishnaabeg Re-Creation, Resurgence, and a New Emergence*
(Winnipeg: Arbeiter Ring Press, 2011), 32.

46 Luam Kidane and Jarrett Martineau, "Building
Connections across Decolonization Struggles," *ROAR*,
October 29, 2013, https://roarmag.org/essays/
african-indigenous-struggle-decolonization.

47 Harsha Walia, "Decolonizing Together: Moving beyond
a Politics of Solidarity toward a Practice of Decolonization,"
Briarpatch, January 1, 2012, https://briarpatchmagazine.com/
articles/view/decolonizing-together.

48 Coulthard, interview by carla bergman and Nick
Montgomery.

49 Friedrich Wilhelm Nietzsche, *Thus Spake Zarathustra: A
Book for All and None*, trans. Thomas Wayne (New York: Algora
Publishing, 2003), 42.

50 Coulthard, interview by carla bergman and Nick
Montgomery.

51 Mingus, "On Collaboration."

52 Simpson, interview by Nick Montgomery and carla
bergman.

Chapter 3: Trust and Responsibility as Common Notions

1 Ursula K. LeGuin, "Ursula K. Le Guin's Speech at National Book Awards: 'Books Aren't Just Commodities,'" *Guardian*, November 20, 2014, https://www.theguardian.com/books/2014/nov/20/ursula-k-le-guin-national-book-awards-speech.

2 crow, *Black Flags and Windmills: Hope, Anarchy, and the Common Ground Collective*, 173.

3 adrienne maree brown, "That Would Be Enough," adriennemareebrown.net, September 6, 2016, http://adriennemareebrown.net/2016/09/06/that-would-be-enough.

4 VOID Network, "VOID Network on the December 2008 Insurrection in Greece," B.A.S.T.A.R.D. Conference, University of California, Berkeley, March 14, 2010, https://www.indybay.org/newsitems/2010/03/18/18641710.php.

5 Sitrin, interview by Nick Montgomery and carla bergman.

6 Many works within this current remain untranslated into English; however, there are a few English sources. In particular, we learned a lot from Sebastian Touza's PhD dissertation and our interview with him. See Colectivo Situaciones, *19&20: Notes for a New Social Protagonism*, trans. Nate Holdren and Sebastian Touza (New York: Minor Compositions, 2012); Deleuze, "Lecture on Spinoza's Concept of Affect"; Marta Malo de Molina, "Common Notions, Part 1: Workers-Inquiry, Co-Research, Consciousness-Raising," *European Institute for Progressive Cultural Policies*, April 2004, http://eipcp.net/transversal/0406/malo/en; Marta Malo de Molina:, "Common Notions, Part 2: Institutional Analysis, Participatory Action-Research, Militant Research," *European Institute for Progressive Cultural Policies*,

April 2004, http://eipcp.net/transversal/0707/malo/en; Touza, "Antipedagogies for Liberation Politics, Consensual Democracy and Post-Intellectual Interventions"; Touza, interview by carla bergman and Nick Montgomery.

7 Touza, "Antipedagogies for Liberation Politics, Consensual Democracy and Post-Intellectual Interventions," 210.

8 Nora Samaran, "On Gaslighting: Dating Tips for the Feminist Man," June 28, 2016, https://norasamaran .com/2016/06/28/on-gaslighting.

9 Matt Hern, "The Promise of Deschooling," *Social Anarchism* 25 (1998), http://library.nothingness.org/articles/SI/ en/display_printable/130.

10 Toby Rollo, "Feral Children: Settler Colonialism, Progress, and the Figure of the Child," *Settler Colonial Studies* (June 2016), 1–20.

11 Gilles Deleuze, "Postscript on the Societies of Control," *October* 59 (1992), 3–7.

12 Institute for Precarious Consciousness, "We Are All Very Anxious," WeArePlanC.org, April 4, 2014, http://www. weareplanc.org/blog/we-are-all-very-anxious.

13 Sitrin, *Everyday Revolutions*, 37.

14 Ivan Illich, *Tools for Conviviality* (New York: Harper & Row, 1973), 12.

15 Our readings and understandings of Illich's work, and our understanding of conviviality in particular, is indebted to conversations with friends who either knew Illich personally or worked closely with his ideas, including Gustavo Esteva, Madhu Suri Prakash, Dan Grego, Dana L. Stuchul and Matt Hern.

16 Quoted in Invisible Committee, *To Our Friends*, 232–33.

17 Marina Sitrin, ed., *Horizontalism: Voices of Popular*

Power in Argentina (Oakland: AK Press, 2006); Sitrin, *Everyday Revolutions*.

18 Rebecca Solnit, *A Paradise Built in Hell: The Extraordinary Communities That Arise in Disaster* (New York: Penguin Books, 2009), 2.

19 Ibid., 7.

20 Leanne Simpson, "Dancing the World into Being: A Conversation with Idle No More's Leanne Simpson," *Yes! Magazine*, March 5, 2013, http://www.yesmagazine.org/peace-justice/dancing-the-world-into-being-a-conversation-with-idle-no-more-leanne-simpson.

21 Quoted in Tony Manno, "Unsurrendered," *Yes! Magazine*, 2015, http://reports.yesmagazine.org/unsurrendered.

22 INCITE! Women of Color Against Violence, "INCITE! Critical Resistance Statement," 2001, http://www.incite-national.org/page/incite-critical-resistance-statement.

23 Rachel Zellars and Naava Smolash, "If Black Women Were Free: Part 1," *Briarpatch*, August 16, 2016, http://briarpatch-magazine.com/articles/view/if-black-women-were-free.

24 Victoria Law, "Against Carceral Feminism," *Jacobin*, October 17, 2014, https://www.jacobinmag.com/2014/10/against-carceral-feminism.

25 Creative Interventions, "Toolkit," CreativeInterventions.org, http://www.creative-interventions.org/tools/toolkit.

26 Quoted in carla bergman and Corine Brown, *Common Notions: Handbook Not Required*, 2015.

27 Gustavo Esteva, interview by carla bergman and Nick Montgomery, video, 2012.

28 Kelsey Cham C., Nick Montgomery, and carla bergman, interview by carla bergman and Nick Montgomery, October 26, 2013.

29 Marina Sitrin, "Occupy Trust: The Role of Emotion in the New Movements," *Cultural Anthropology* (February 2013), https://culanth.org/fieldsights/75-occupy-trust-the-role-of-emotion-in-the-new-movements.

30 Gustavo Esteva and Madhu Suri Prakash, *Grassroots Postmodernism: Remaking the Soil of Cultures* (London: Zed Books, 1998), 91.

31 Day, *Gramsci Is Dead*, 200.

32 Zainab Amadahy, *Wielding the Force: The Science of Social Justice*, Smashwords ed. (Zainab Amadahy, 2013), 36.

33 Esteva and Prakash, *Grassroots Postmodernism*, 89.

Chapter 4: Stifling Air, Burnout, Political Performance

1 Amadahy, *Wielding the Force*, 149.

2 Emma Goldman, "The Hypocrisy of Puritanism," in *Red Emma Speaks: An Emma Goldman Reader*, ed. Alix Kates Shulman (Amherst, NY: Humanity Books, 1998), 157.

3 Chris Dixon, "For the Long Haul," *Briarpatch Magazine*, June 21, 2016, http://briarpatchmagazine.com/articles/view/for-the-long-haul.

4 We first encountered the concept of "public secret" as a way of getting at the affect of anxiety today, described by the Institute for Precarious Consciousness. Earlier uses can be traced to the work of Ken Knabb (which credits the concept to Marx) and his curation of Situationist writing, as well as Jean-Pierre Voyer's reading of Reich. See Institute for Precarious Consciousness, "Movement Internationalism(s)," *Interface* 6/2; Jean-Pierre Voyer, "Wilhelm Reich: How to Use," in *Public Secrets*, trans. Ken Knabb (Bureau of Public Secrets, 1997), http://www.bopsecrets.

org/PS/reich.htm; Jean-Pierre Voyer to Ken Knabb, "Discretion Is the Better Part of Value," April 20, 1973, http://www.bopse-crets.org/PS/Reich.add.htm.

5 This was suggested to us by Richard Day.

6 brown, interview by carla bergman and Nick Montgomery.

7 Amador Fernández-Savater, "Reopening the Revolutionary Question," *ROAR Magazine* 0 (December 2015).

8 Federici, interview by carla bergman and Nick Montgomery.

9 Touza, interview by carla bergman and Nick Montgomery.

10 Friedrich Nietzsche, *On the Genealogy of Morals and Ecce Homo*, ed. Walter Kaufmann (New York: Vintage, 1989), 32.

Chapter 5: Undoing Rigid Radicalism, Activating Joy

1 Foucault, "Preface."

2 Cited in Ashanti Alston, "An Interview with Ashanti Alston," interview by Team Colors, June 6, 2008, https://inthemiddleofthewhirlwind.wordpress.com/an-interview-with-ashanti-alston.

3 Thoburn develops his conception of a "militant diagram" through a reading of Deleuze and Guattari, and we have found it useful in thinking about rigid radicalism as an affective tendency that is irreducible to the gestures, habits, practices, and statements that are simultaneously its fuel and its discharge. See Nicholas Thoburn, "Weatherman, the Militant Diagram, and the Problem of Political Passion," *New Formations* 68/1 (2010), 125–42.

4 Colectivo Situaciones, "Something More on Research Militancy: Footnotes and Procedures and (In)Decisions," 5.

5 Thoburn, "Weatherman, the Militant Diagram, and the

Problem of Political Passion," 129; Cathy Wilkerson, *Flying Close to the Sun: My Life and Times as a Weatherman* (New York: Seven Stories Press, 2007), 265–300.

6 Bernardine Dohrn, Bill Ayers, and Jeff Jones, eds., *Sing a Battle Song: The Revolutionary Poetry, Statements, and Communiques of the Weather Underground 1970-1974* (New York: Seven Stories Press, 2006), 18.

7 Bill Ayers, *Fugitive Days: Memoirs of an Antiwar Activist* (Boston: Beacon Press, 2009), 154.

8 Esteva, interview by Nick Montgomery and carla bergman.

9 Thoburn, "Weatherman, the Militant Diagram, and the Problem of Political Passion," 134.

10 Esteva, interview by Nick Montgomery and carla bergman.

11 Sitrin, interview by Nick Montgomery and carla bergman.

12 Emma Goldman, *Living My Life* (New York: Dover Publications, 1970), 54.

13 amory starr, "Grumpywarriorcool: What Makes Our Movements White?," in *Igniting a Revolution: Voices in Defense of the Earth* (Oakland: AK Press, 2006), 379.

14 Ibid., 383.

15 crow, *Black Flags and Windmills*, 81.

16 Alston, interview by Nick Montgomery and carla bergman.

17 Richard J. F. Day, interview by Nick Montgomery and carla bergman, phone, March 18, 2014.

18 Alston, interview by Nick Montgomery and carla bergman.

19 CrimethInc., "Against Ideology?," CrimethInc.com, 2010, http://www.crimethinc.com/texts/atoz/ideology.php.

20 Erich Fromm, *Man for Himself: An Inquiry into the Psychology of Ethics* (Oxon: Routledge, 1947), 235.

21 See Raoul Vaneigem, *The Movement of the Free Spirit*, trans. Randall Cherry and Ian Patterson, rev. ed. (New York, Cambridge, MA: Zone Books, 1998); Federici, *Caliban and the Witch*, 21–60.

22 Nietzsche, *On the Genealogy of Morals and Ecce Homo*, 33.

23 Ibid., 36.

24 Quoted by Maya Angelou in Malcolm X, *Malcolm X: An Historical Reader*, ed. James L. Conyers and Andrew P. Smallwood (Durham: Carolina Academic Press, 2008), 181.

25 Kelsey Cham C., "Radical Language in the Mainstream," *Perspectives on Anarchist Theory* 29 (2016), 122–23.

26 Asam Ahmad, "A Note on Call-Out Culture," *Briarpatch*, March 2, 2015, http://briarpatchmagazine.com/articles/view/a-note-on-call-out-culture.

27 Ngọc Loan Trân, "Calling IN: A Less Disposable Way of Holding Each Other Accountable," *Black Girl Dangerous*, December 18, 2013, http://www.blackgirldangerous.org/2013/12/calling-less-disposable-way-holding-accountable.

28 Ibid.

29 Chris Crass, "White Supremacy Cannot Have Our People: For a Working Class Orientation at the Heart of White Anti-Racist Organizing," *Medium*, July 28, 2016, https://medium.com/@chriscrass/white-supremacy-cannot-have-our-people-21e87d2b268a.

30 Ibid.

31 Ursula Le Guin, *The Lathe of Heaven* (New York: Scribner, 1999), 137.

32 This section title is borrowed from Eve Sedgwick, from

whom we've also taken the concept of paranoid reading. See Eve Kosofsky Sedgwick, "Paranoid Reading and Reparative Reading, or, You're so Paranoid, You Probably Think This Essay Is about You," in *Touching Feeling: Affect, Pedagogy, Performativity* (Durham: Duke University Press, 2003), 124–51.

33 Killjoy, interview by carla bergman and Nick Montgomery.

34 Sedgwick, "Paranoid Reading and Reparative Reading, or, You're so Paranoid, You Probably Think This Essay Is about You."

35 Day, interview by Nick Montgomery and carla bergman.

36 Mik Turje, interview by Nick Montgomery and carla bergman, March 4, 2014.

37 Hasan Shakur was a prison abolition and anti-violence organizer and prisoner who worked with Imarisha. As she explains in her book, he was on death row for nine years before he was executed on August 31, 2006, in Huntsville Prison.

38 Walidah Imarisha, *Angels with Dirty Faces: Three Stories of Crime, Prison, and Redemption* (Oakland: AK Press, 2016), 113–15.

39 Walidah Imarisha, interview by Nick Montgomery and carla bergman, email, December 22, 2015.

40 Federici, interview by Nick Montgomery and carla bergman.

Outro

1 John Holloway, *Change the World without Taking Power: The Meaning of Revolution Today*, 2nd rev. ed. (London: Pluto Press, 2005), 215.

2 Coulthard, interview by Nick Montgomery and carla bergman.

3 This turn of phrase comes to us from Stevphen Shukaitis's wonderful book *Imaginal Machines: Autonomy and Self-Organization in the Revolutions of Everyday Life* (New York: Autonomedia, 2009), 141–42, http://www.minorcompositions.info/wp-content/uploads/2009/10/ImaginalMachines-web.pdf.

4 This idea is paraphrased from Lauren Berlant and her conception of "cruel optimism," a relation in which our attachments become obstacles to our flourishing. See Lauren Berlant, *Cruel Optimism* (Durham: Duke University Press, 2011).

5 Federici, interview by Nick Montgomery and carla bergman.

6 Zainab Amadahy, interview by Nick Montgomery and carla bergman, January 15, 2016.

Appendix 1: Feeling Powers Growing—An Interview with Silvia Federici

1 Note: when we interviewed Silvia Federici, we were still using the phrase "sad militancy" in place of "rigid radicalism." The original terminology is retained throughout.

2 Jo Freeman, "Trashing: The Dark Side of Sisterhood," JoFreeman.com, n.d., http://www.jofreeman.com/joreen/trashing.htm.

3 Marge Piercy, *The Grand Coolie Dam*, (Boston: New England Free Press, 1969).

4 See Jo Freeman, "The Tyranny of Structurelessness," *Ms. Magazine*, July 1973.

5 Silvia Federici, "Putting Feminism Back on Its Feet," *Social Text* 9/10 (1984), 338–46.

6 See Raúl Zibechi, *Dispersing Power: Social Movements as Anti-State Forces*, trans. Ramor Ryan (Oakland: AK Press, 2010);

Zibechi, *Territories in Resistance*.

7 Silvia Federici, "Losing the Sense That We Can Do Something Is the Worst Thing That Can Happen," interview by Candida Hadley, Halifax Media Co-op, November 5, 2013, http://halifax.mediacoop.ca/audio/losing-sense-we-can-do-something-worst-thing-can-h/19601.

Index

Institute for Anarchist Studies

The IAS, a nonprofit foundation established in 1996, aims to support the development of anarchism by supporting politically engaged scholarship that explores social domination and reconstructive visions of a free society. All IAS projects strive to encourage public intellectuals and promote collective self-reflection within revolutionary movements. To this end, the IAS has funded nearly a hundred projects by authors from numerous countries, including Argentina, Lebanon, Canada, Chile, Ireland, Nigeria, Germany, South Africa, and the United States. It also publishes the journal Perspectives on Anarchist Theory and collaborates on this book series, among other projects. The IAS is part of a larger movement seeking to create a nonhierarchical society. It is internally democratic and works in solidarity with people around the globe who share its values. The IAS is completely supported by donations from anarchists and other anti-authoritarians—like you—and/or their projects, with any contributions exclusively funding grants and IAS operating expenses; for more information or to contribute to the work of the IAS, see http://www.anarchist-studies.org/.

AK Press

AK Press is a worker-run collective that publishes and distributes radical books, visual and audio media, and other material. We work long hours for short money because we believe in what we do. We're anarchists, which is reflected both in the books we provide and the way we organize our business. Decisions at AK Press are made collectively, from what we publish, to what we distribute, and how we structure our labor. The work, from sweeping floors to answering phones, is shared. When the telemarketers call and ask, "who's in charge?" the answer is: everyone. Our goal is supplying radical words and images to as many people as possible. We ensure these materials are widely available to help you make positive (or hell, revolutionary) changes in the world. For more information on AK Press, or to place an order, see http://www.akpress.org/.

Justseeds Artists' Cooperative

Justseeds Artists' Cooperative is a decentralized community of twenty-nine artists who have banded together to distribute their work as well as collaborate with and support each other. We regularly produce graphics and culture for social justice movements, much of which we distribute for free on our website. We believe in the power of personal expression in concert with collective action to transform society. For more information on Justseeds Artists' Cooperative or to order work, see http://www.justseeds.org/.

Anarchist Interventions Series

AK Press is small, in terms of staff and resources, but we also manage to be one of the world's most productive anarchist publishing houses. We publish close to twenty books every year, and distribute thousands of other titles published by like-minded independent presses and projects from around the globe. We're entirely worker-run and democratically managed. We operate without a corporate structure—no boss, no managers, no bullshit.

The Friends of AK program is a way you can directly contribute to the continued existence of AK Press, and ensure that we're able to keep publishing books like this one! Friends pay $25 a month directly into our publishing account ($30 for Canada, $35 for international), and receive a copy of every book AK Press publishes for the duration of their membership! Friends also receive a discount on anything they order from our website or buy at a table: 50% on AK titles, and 20% on everything else. We have a Friends of AK ebook program as well: $15 a month gets you an electronic copy of every book we publish for the duration of your membership. You can even sponsor a very discounted membership for someone in prison.

Email friendsofak@akpress.org for more info, or visit the Friends of AK Press website: https://www.akpress.org/friends.html

There are always great book projects in the works—so sign up now to become a Friend of AK Press, and let the presses roll!